Still, Still, Green Bananas

Still, Still, Green Bananas

CAROL RAE LEVERGOOD

Still, Still, Green Bananas

Copyright © 2024 Carol Rae Levergood.

Published in Springfield, MO by Tribune Publishing.

No part of this book may be reproduced, stored in a retrieval system, or transmitted in any form or by any means, electronic, mechanical, photocopying, recording, or otherwise, without express written permission of the publisher.

Scripture quotations are taken from the King James Version, The Holy Bible—public domain.

ISBN-13: 978-1-962596-15-2 (eBook)
ISBN-13: 978-1-962596-14-5 (Paperback)

Cover design by Randy Harp

DEDICATION

I would like to dedicate this book to my beloved husband, Bill, whose love, care, and sense of humor guided our family through so many difficult times. Bill was always an inspiration to us, deeply devoted to the Lord and His work. His patience and steadfastness during our ripening seasons as a family were a gift we will always cherish. Like a bunch of green bananas, we ripened together, each of us maturing at our own pace. We would not trade the privilege of growing together with him. Thank you, Bill, for being part of that journey.

Though Bill passed away on May 29th, 2024, and is profoundly missed, his influence remains woven into every part of my life, including this book. His support and encouragement have shaped so much of what I've written. Several of my books, which he played an integral role in, will be published in time as finances allow. I am deeply grateful for the kindness and support I've received during this season of loss. Bill would be amazed, though not surprised, by the incredible goodness of God, and I know he would be proud of our children and of whom they have become in the Lord.

CONTENTS

	Acknowledgments	I
	Introduction	3
1	No Sagging Rainbows	9
2	Plunge of Faith	17
3	Me Fearful? I'm A Frayed Knot	25
4	At Peace or In Pieces	35
5	No Shortcuts	43
6	Pressure Pan Dilemma	49
7	Your Way or Mine	55
8	Life is Full of Surprises	61
9	Making Memories	71
10	Trolls, Giants, and Mountains	87
11	Termites, Bats, Frogs, and More	95
	About the Author: Who is the Banana Lady?	115

ACKNOWLEDGMENTS

I would like to acknowledge two very special people whose influence and support have meant so much to me.

First, I want to express my deep appreciation to Pamela McCord. The title of this book was born out of a memorable conversation we had about green bananas and their slow but inevitable ripening process. That conversation left such an impression on me that I began placing pictures of green bananas around my home as a reminder that maturity—both for myself, my children, and others—will come in time. Pam's friendship has been a blessing over the years, whether through phone calls, long letters, emails, or Facebook messages that have kept us connected across the miles. Her compassion for the Brazilian people and her family's love for Brazil have been a source of inspiration in my own life. God has used Pam's heart for missions to influence me more than once. Thank you, Pam, for your unwavering friendship and the profound impact you've had on my journey.

I would also like to extend my heartfelt thanks to Randy Harp, a dear friend, fellow writer, and the dedicated publisher and editor of this revised edition of *Still, Still Green Bananas*. His unwavering support, expertise, and encouragement have been invaluable throughout this process. Thank you, Randy, for your friendship and for helping to bring this book to life.

INTRODUCTION

Still, Still Green Bananas

Looking out my window, I see that a plastic bag and strong winds are the perfect combination for what I have felt inside at times. I watched the plastic carry-all whip around through the branches, unable to loosen from the fingered branch that held it captive.

Hours later, I noticed it still there, struggling less fiercely, flattened strips no longer ballooned. There was just enough evidence to show it was a grocery bag of sorts. I was so much like that bag: thrown, tossed, unable to fend for myself. My flesh warred with the spirit, but why? Why had I tried to war against the flesh?

I knew I had no strength of my own, but finally exhausted, I cried to the Lord, my Defender and Deliverer. Once again, I rested where I should have long ago, in the arms of the Almighty... and slept. Why did I wait till I was exhausted? I must have shown very little evidence of being one of God's own during that struggle.

As a missionary, little did I know that I was a lot like the green bananas that hung from the tall stalks in our backyard in Pouso Alegre, Minas Gerais, Brazil. Sometimes, we placed freshly picked green bananas in the dark pantry to ripen faster and to keep them from the persistent peck of the birds. My dear friend Pam and I would compare these green, soon-to-be luscious fruits to our children growing up.

My husband, Bill, even suggested we place our two children in the pantry to ripen and mature faster. As I saw Bill leaning against the pantry door and hints of the children inside laughing and hollering at their dad, I knew he meant business.

Jokingly, of course, I begged for mercy on their behalf, knowing they would mature in time even though, at this instance, it didn't seem like they would; they're children, not fully grown yet. They had a reason for their immaturity; I didn't.

At this incident, I was reminded that part of the growing process is watching and working together to see that maturity come to light, no matter how painful that process might be. Then, I began to see that each one of us—our children, our spouse, a friend, or a member of the family or congregation—will mature at different times.

To ripen properly, green bananas need a tropical climate with the right amount of sun and rain and well-prepared, fertile ground. A good balance is needed, or we'll stay green and grainy, just like the bananas placed in the pantry.

In front of the marketplace in the city of Pouso Alegre, there sat a beggar asking for money from the passersby. An open wound ran from the ankle to his knee. I had seen him many times, and each time, I felt sick at the display. For months into years, he was there, and his leg never healed. We were told medical help had been offered him, but he chose to earn his living on the sympathy of others. Eventually, he lost his leg to gangrene.

Are you holding on to past hurts? They only bring you pain, but God can help you pick up the pieces even when you have blown it or others make you feel you have blown it. There is a difference.

If you are hurting today, I encourage you to read this book and, of course, look for someone who would be a good mentor for godly advice. What happens when we keep scraping our wounds daily to make them more grotesque, scraping our hurts, disappointments, and failed expectations? We never let them heal, and we decide to live as if we were wounded yesterday. Scraping our wounds occupies every waking moment and then some. It saps our very own strength and energy. The beggar in the marketplace had a choice, and he chose to keep scraping his wound all for greed. Do not wait till you are overwhelmed as I did. You are not alone on the path to healing.

I walked outside to the most beautiful flower, which opened with the morning dew and the warm sunlight as if it were stretching and flexing like I do, trying to wake up. An appropriate name for this flower is—the Rose of Sharon. But these are here for such a short time, though beautiful and rich in color. There is one next to it that is faded away and ready to fall off. This morning, reading from 1 Peter, this verse was so appropriate. I smiled as I thought of our True Rose of Sharon—Jesus Christ himself—and fadeth not away—He is everlasting. Think on those things, not the hurts that take you down.

"For all flesh is as grass, and all the glory of man as the flower of grass. The grass withereth, and the flower thereof falleth away. But the word of the Lord endureth forever…" 1 Peter 1:24

Still, Still Green Bananas

CHAPTER ONE:
NO SAGGING RAINBOWS

Still, Still Green Bananas

May 1974 began a very exciting time for Bill and me as we were going up for approval as missionaries to Brazil. Unanimously voted on, we immediately began 18 months of deputation. I am not sure 2 ½-year-old April understood what we were doing as we dragged her state to state, church to church to raise support. But April traveled well, which sure made it easier.

Two years prior, we worked at the Wick Road Baptist Church in Taylor, Michigan, under Bernie Rogers. What a great experience working under his leadership and great preaching. Then, just before approval, Bill and I worked on staff at the Cherry Street Baptist Church, where Harold Brown pastored at the time and where Ken D. Gillming and Ken E. Gillming continued to pastor. Both of these churches were our home churches.

We met and befriended some wonderful godly pastors and church members while on our travels. But our first time to meet a pastor was, at times, stressful as we prayed and hoped for that desperately needed support. New and green, we were scared. Little did we know the ripening process had already been initiated.

Our permanent visas arrived at Christmas of 1975, and on the twelfth of January, Bill's birthday, we loaded a U-Haul. We said goodbye to my family that night, and the next day, January 13, we said goodbye to my sister, Beverly, and John at 5:00 in the morning. Rain fell in sheets, and darkness shrouded the early morning hours. We drove away, watching and waving till we could no longer see the small shadow of a figure in the doorway.

Silence fell heavy as we stared down the highway in a curtain of wet darkness. We felt heaviness inside, weighing as much as the silence and the torrent rain together. The overcast of gloominess in the air was profound as we journeyed toward the unknown, the unknown we had been working on for many months.

As we drove away that day, I was saying in the flesh, "Lord, You could have given us a beautiful day to leave our loved ones." As I was feeling sorry for myself, scared of what lay ahead, and brooding over the weather, I began feeling a big knot in my throat. Then, all of a sudden, the clouds parted, and the sun broke through. It was as if the Lord was saying, "I know how heavy your heart is and how confused you might be. Trust Me! Everything will be all right." We then had a beautiful, calm ride with 3½-year-old April seated between us, snuggling close as if she understood it all.

We finally arrived in New Orleans to ship our things, but we still had three days to wait for our flight to Brazil. After shipping our belongings and doing the embassy work, the only thing left was to wait…

Sitting in our motel room, I began to think about the unknown and already missing everyone, when suddenly I was overwhelmed with panic that nearly paralyzed me for the next two days. It was just the last-minute jitters intensified. That was my first, but far from last, confrontation with panic.

As missionaries, we are many times afraid to express apprehensions for fear that others will find us weak. If God called me, I shouldn't feel these things. That is why I hid much of what I was feeling. But why then did God ask Isaiah to write verses like Isaiah 41:10-13? Jill Briscoe explains in her book from many years ago, "How to Follow the Shepherd," that we will experience "reasonable and unreasonable fears," those exaggerated by Satan himself. I realized I had allowed my imagination to run wild and gave room for Satan to roam my thoughts and fears. At that moment, I gave them to the Lord. What freedom!

I was able to pull myself together and call home one more time before leaving the States. I could tell Bill was very nervous about the details of everything and the unknown. The day for actually heading to Brazil arrived. South America, here we come.

◆◆◆◆◆

Brazil. The sound of unfamiliar language, samba music, and traffic that would boggle anyone's mind hit us as we landed on this foreign soil, the soil God called us to. Bill and I were certainly young and green upon our arrival, but tropical Brazil would change that over time.

We began to love so many things about this Portuguese-speaking country. Besides the people, we loved the food. April loved the warm French bread, and we all loved the fresh fruits and vegetables all year round. Bill and I enjoyed the rich coffee and café over time and began to prefer it above the American brew. Brown beans and rice, or black beans with meat called feijoada, also accompanied by rice, became our favorite dishes. My mother visited us with Norma and Kenneth Gillming (from Cherry Street Baptist—our sending church), and her favorite meal was also the feijoada dish.

Surprisingly, we enjoyed their pizzas with the variety of tuna and onion topped with mozzarella cheese, sardine in a tomato sauce and mozzarella, French fries and mozzarella, and their California pizza made with Canadian bacon, fruit, and mozzarella. We didn't much care for the peas and creamed corn, not our style.

After language study and a short furlough, we headed for Pouso Alegre, in the state of Minas Gerais. Our dear friends from the city of Campinas, Pastor Claudette, and Margarida, influenced us greatly in this area, especially concerned about Margarida's unsaved family. Margarida came from a family of 20-some brothers and sisters.

Margarida loved the Lord, and when we went back to the States for that short furlough, God laid it on our hearts to give her our washing machine. Looking at her constant open sores on her hands from hand-washing her family's clothes led us to feel compassion for her, a pastor's wife and friend. She used that machine for many, many years, never failing to thank us every time she saw us. What a blessing! Years later, Claudette was killed on that very highway that took us all on our survey trip to meet their family; shortly after, Margarida died.

The Lord knew what He was doing, of course, when He called us to the state of Minas Gerais. This state is comparable to the state of Wisconsin because of its dairy and beef products. Most of all, we loved the Minas (pronounced Mee-nes) people who, at first, were distrusting souls but, in time, opened their homes and hearts to us. I am sure we were strange to them, the only Americans living in the town of 50,000, which grew over time to 150,000. The Mineiros were not sure why we were there. In other ways, it felt like we were in the Show Me state. Little did we know we would fall in love with Pouso Alegre and the nearby town of Ouro Fino.

In time, the Lord led us to build a youth camp 5 miles outside Pouso Alegre. The work was going well, souls were coming to the Lord, and the need for a youth camp was very vital. There was nothing attractive about the land that spread out like a thrown quilt at the foot of the mountain. But the mountain held my attention. This is it! This is my mountain. I thought this was the biggest mountain I would ever have to face in my lifetime, but I was wrong.

The rugged land with no trees would need to be tamed, presenting a challenge we gladly took on, and in the end, would prove to be worth the effort because it was not going to be built through our strength alone. We claimed that mountain, and from afar, we knew we were close to home when it came into view. The children would say, "There's your mountain, Mom!" We didn't actually own the mountain, and of course, it wasn't on our property, but God placed it there for us to enjoy. I claimed it as my own!

God's beautiful mountain and vivid rainbows seemed to encourage us when we were downhearted. Whether light rains or downpours, rainbows always seemed to appear beginning on one end of the property and ending on the far side of the land. Single and sometimes double rainbows appeared in the sky. Wow! We have our own personal rainbows. This all seemed so much more than I could have ever dreamed of. Bill and I together named the youth project "Camp Rainbow!" My heart aches to think how the world uses the rainbow to mean other things, but God's Word used it first, and it will continue to be Camp Rainbow, after God's own heart.

The most exciting aspect of the rainbow is that when I look upon it, God is also looking upon it. Read Genesis 9:13-17, but especially verse 16: "And the bow shall be in the cloud; and I will look upon it, that I may remember the everlasting covenant between God and every living creature of all flesh that is upon the earth."

A friend of ours, Dan Wells, visited us for three months and was about to return to the U.S. when he said, "I haven't seen one of those rainbows you've talked so much about." We realized he was right. Raining only in the night gave no opportunity for a rainbow to be seen. The day before he left, rain fell over the mountain, which was perfect for a rainbow. Sure enough, beside the chapel, a multi-hued rainbow filled the sky. The color-filled sky seemed so close to the veranda that we just wanted to reach out and touch the misty colors.

Many times during camp, I would have liked to have controlled the weather. Isn't that prideful, trying to play God as if He doesn't know what He is doing? I wanted so much to have perfect camps, with perfect weather, so the young people could go home talking about the wonderful time they had.

Where do I come up with the idea that sunshine is the only thing that brings a good camp? I thank the Lord there are still some things we can't put our sticky fingers on or have control over. Sometimes, those rainy days are meant to be they are very important in God's plan. It's sometimes more profitable if campers have a few hours in the dorms to sing, talk, encourage, or be counseled.

God has a purpose for everything, and when I took my hands off from trying to manipulate God or the weather, I began to enjoy our ministry more. I enjoy painting, but I cannot even imagine trying to paint a rainbow; that is one thing God alone can do and do it perfectly; mine would certainly sag somewhere.

There are no sagging, drooping, multi-hued arches when God is in control. When our Creator does something, He does it well, like placing these beauties perfectly where He wants them and when God wants them. For some things, we just need to take our hands off and let Him have control. He truly knows what He is doing.

Thank you, Father, for the fact you make no "sagging rainbows."

Rainbows

For a rainbow to exist
Two items are a must.
First, there is the rain that falls
Then, the sun in its full thrust.

Unfading and faithful,
If that's the way we wish to be,
Must first be showered with downpours
Of life's uncertainties.

Causing us to draw from the abundance of God's love
Feeling penetrating rays from the True light from above.

Without the presence of God's Son
We'd have no rainbows in our lives,
Just trials would exist
With no relief in sight.

So…the rain and the Son
Are a must, we will agree,
To be the kind of Christian,
Christ wants us to be.

May we show forth the same true colors
That stand so vivid and so true,
And may we serve a purpose,
O Father, be more like you.

CHAPTER TWO: PLUNGE OF FAITH

Still, Still Green Bananas

Bill and I needed a plunger for the kitchen sink after just a few weeks in Brazil. Not knowing Portuguese well enough our dictionary became our life saver, most of the time. Bill did what he always did, looked up the word plunger in the English dictionary, but there were several words for plunger in the Portuguese, so he went eenie-meenie-minie-moe and chose the first word written. Assuming it was the most correct definition, he was armed and ready to go.

Bill hoped to find a plunger and not have to ask anyone, but not taking a chance, had the word written down. After looking around, he found no such thing, so he mustered up enough courage to ask a store clerk. He had practiced the pronunciation and said it near perfect. Approaching the clerk, he said in broken Portuguese that he needed a "mergulhador" and even tried demonstrating what he needed, but the clerk sent him to another area to ask. "Must not be her department," he thought.

Going to another department, Bill asked again if they had a "mergulhador." She didn't know what he meant, so he even used sign language, making the swishing, sucking sound of the plunger when a sink is stopped up with water. He was sent to yet another clerk.

Realizing he was being sent around the store as the joke of the day, he came home disappointed and discouraged without a plunger. By then, I had solved the problem in the sink using my hand as a suction cup. He wasn't sure if he was happy or mad that I had taken care of it while he was suffering humiliation at the hands of the clerks. He did demonstrate the function or sucking sound of a plunger and the hand gestures that accompanied it very well, I must say.

We both finally began to laugh about the dilemma and laugh a lot we have over the years. The story of our first days of learning the language is still told today. By the way, the word for plunger is 'disintupidor' in case you ever need one while you visit beautiful Brazil. If you ask for a 'mergulhador' you will be asking for a person who plunges into things headfirst. Bill figured out that he must have been asking for the Tidy bowl man to plunge into his sink and clean it out. They must have been out of them that day.

A few years later, I found a Precious Moments figurine to remember that moment. This little girl was running with a plunger in her hands. On the bottom of the figurine, it says, "Faith Takes a Plunge." That said it all!

It took a plunge of faith for Bill and me to return to Brazil for a second term, knowing Bill might not see his mother again. Leukemia was taking its toll. The day arrived for us to head back to Brazil. We said our goodbyes and, driving away, we waved till we could no longer see her fragile body as she stood waving back on her front porch in Taylor, Michigan. Her champagne-colored wig covered what was left of her once vibrant red hair while tears stained her face. Her dream was to visit her son in Brazil before the Lord took her home, but she knew that might not happen.

Six months into our second term back in Brazil, Bill received a call from Bro. Bill Sears to come home because his mother did not have much time to live. Florence Snowburger Levergood hung on until Bill arrived. Knowing he was coming perked up her spirits a bit. Florence knew why her son was in Brazil, but she still missed him terribly. She also knew that the only reason he would come home was that she was going to die soon. She hung on to see her son one more time. Sandra, Bill, and Dad stood around her, enjoying each other in their final goodbyes as she slipped into a coma and eventually went on to be with the Lord. Rev. Leland Kennedy and Bill Sears did her home-going service, the pastors she loved so much.

Leaving family was never easy for either of us. For me, I would picture my dad coming up on his motorcycle down the dirt road towards our house on the camp. Like in the States, I pictured him riding up and asking me if I had a fresh pot of coffee on. If I did, he'd want a cup, or I would insist on making some just to sit with him a while.

Certain areas of Brazil, smells, or crafts took my mind back to Mom. I thought of times my grandmother would make a basket lunch for my family of eight to eat on our way up to the Upper Peninsula of Michigan, past the "Straits of Mackinaw." Their mom had us pile out of the car on a lush part of a grassy field. We would run up and down with her to run off some energy, but only after we had fresh tomatoes, ham, and bread with fresh raspberries and cookies she made in her wonderful kitchen. Our trips to the Upper Peninsula were trips to remember.

The most precious of memories cannot be bought. These are the ones we have taken time to cultivate, sometimes without even our knowledge of doing so as a family. Maybe it was that evening playing a game with the family and laughing till your side hurt. The memories I seem to cherish now were small stuff, those I took for granted to not be much or very important, but in the end were special.

On the field, we make our own memories with our children when the family is not around, like grandparents, aunts, and uncles. It takes a plunge of faith to leave loved ones, but when we do God's will, we can be content and happy where God calls us.

Anything that is a change from our normal daily lives can bring on fear, fear of being able to adapt. It might be a small change of moving across town or a big change when your boss sends you packing after 20 years for downsizing. A new location, job, profession, new school, and new relationships, just to name a few, cause fear in all of us.

In my life, there have been quite a few changes.

The idea of a foreign field I loved, but in my heart, it felt permanent, and emotionally I was not quite ready to think that way. I have to take things in small doses and find I love change, but I thought too far ahead, too large, and not one day at a time like Jesus said. My emotions seemed to bluster and bristle at the final moment of leaving New Orleans.

Fear stepped in, and I gave place to doubts about whether I could be the missionary everyone expected me to be or let everyone down who was counting on me. I realized many years later the fear of failure and rejection were always lurking, waiting for a small opening to defeat me.

Changes started with college, married life adjustments, a move back to Michigan, an Associate Pastorate Internship, visiting churches as a new missionary, a new field of Brazil, and a new language, and eventually, back home after 21 years as a missionary.

Some changes are good, some are easy, some are forced upon us, some are because of bad decisions in our lives, and some take a real plunge of faith. We must be adaptable, not just as missionaries but as

Christians. Count on changes in this ever-changing world.

Little did I know God was preparing me a "Michigander."

I was saved in Michigan, and when we moved to Springfield, Missouri, I went forward for assurance and was baptized by Kenneth Gillming Sr. Since our house and the garage used for services for the Airwood Baptist at the time didn't have a baptismal, I was baptized along with some of my sisters and brothers at Seminole Baptist one afternoon.

I was born in Michigan and raised in Missouri, but I grew up in Brazil. God had reasons for moving Lloyd and Velma Stearns and their six children to Missouri. We all have great memories of the house where Cherry Street Baptist saw its' start. Growing up with Ginger, Keith, Kenny, and Mark Gillming was sure a lot of fun, too, running back and forth between their house and ours through the woods.

What a change it was: married life with Bill. Deeply in love, I inherited not only this "knight in shining armor," but I also gained a Pennsylvanian background. The colloquial expression, "Did you red up your room?" was quite interesting to say the least, as well as getting used to my new German name, Levergood. I inherited a love for the Detroit Tigers, Lions, Pistons, and the Red Wings.

Now, I really took to the Detroit Tigers in the '70s and took my Walkman while I was jogging so I wouldn't miss a game. People must have thought I was a bit strange when jogging along and jumping for joy at a home run. It was the arm pulled back celebrating with a definite "yes" for "all right!" This just brought back a lot of memories of my Grandpa Stearns listening to games on the radio and Granny Hill, who loved watching the Detroit Tigers on TV.

All these changes were healthy and exciting, and my world opened up to new opportunities I had never dreamed of. Changes will occur; nothing stays the same. Those changes require a plunge of faith. Bathe decisions with prayer before making any move, but if the door opens, go for it. We need to be still and patiently wait for that without a doubt assurance from God and be really careful not to make a decision based on emotions.

If we had not taken the "plunge of faith," look at what wonderful people, times, and events we would have missed. What blessings are you missing out on by not taking that "plunge of faith?" Remember to make sure that there is an open door, or the ordeal could end up more than a plunge, flat on your face.

Still, Still Green Bananas

CHAPTER 3:
ME FEARFUL?
I'M A FRAYED KNOT

Still, Still Green Bananas

Why do we believe some scriptures are for the neighbor or someone else and certainly not for us? God couldn't be talking to me. We know the Bible says life is as a vapor, but when someone we know dies, it is as though the concept is all brand new. I have secretly bargained with God, not openly, but in my heart and thoughts: "No, God! That's not fair," or "Take me, if necessary, but please don't touch my children!" Life in this sin-filled world is not easy; in fact, it is just plain tough. We don't understand and won't completely on this earth.

> *"For now we see through a glass, darkly; but then face to face: now I know in part; but then shall I know even as also I am known."* **I Corinthians 13:12**

I do not always show my suffering to others until it overwhelms me. We each have to go through pain and hurt, and no one can do it for us. Total dependency on God is necessary at this point. When you have exhausted all others at hearing your woes as I have, and it still hurts, it may be because that is not how you and I are to be free of our burdens. Only God is made to carry our pain and worries. With others, we are to be compassionate and help where we are able, but we are not made to carry the burdens of the world; God is.

Let your children know you are there for them, and then truly be there. That doesn't mean bail out continually, but emotionally helping your children find solutions to their concerns or situations. As parents, we need to recognize when we have made mistakes, admitting errors to the child whether young or in adulthood. This helps them see us in a different light and as humans instead of giving them the idea we think we're perfect and make no mistakes.

Learn to forgive yourself after you have asked forgiveness for your recognized failures. Each of these steps is necessary to heal hurt. Give your children to the Lord, allowing Him to work just as He must do in you. Be truthful and transparent; you might as well, as they're going to see through you anyway. Extra baggage carried around will get you nowhere, and even slow the process of healing to a halt.

When I hit rock bottom with a serious chemical deficit, I lost 20 lbs. within two weeks and suffered severe anxiety and deep depression. Dr. Geraldo from the main work came to see me and explained that I would need some help getting back on my feet. I hid under the covers with embarrassment. In love for me, he said, "Carol, let's talk. You need medication to get the chemicals back in order, and when the physical is back on track, the emotional will follow suit."

When too much stress or situations hit at one time, and we become overwhelmed, this is called situational depression. Fear, which I did not realize, had filled my heart after the mafia had hit our house, and several of our Brazilian family members were tragically killed on the highways, including an 8-year-old boy we loved so dearly.

One day, I went to the marketplace to buy a few days' supplies of fruit and vegetables, and as I was walking in, I realized something all of a sudden was happening to the right of me. The woman arm's length from me was just crushed under the back wheel of the dump truck that had come up on the sidewalk to gather the market waste. The crowd panicked, and I, without even thinking, ran to help lift her and place her in a van that was willing to make a run to the hospital. It was too late; the woman died on the way. I stared at the scene for the longest time, trying to put together what had just happened. The images stayed in my mind, and a feeling of helplessness filled my heart.

While we were home on furlough, our house was robbed of nearly everything we owned except two barrels of family memories chained together, too heavy for them to lift. We went back to an empty home. There is something about someone uninvited intruding into your house and home, whether you were present or not.

So many things happened, one right after another, and finally, an overload came big time. I didn't see it coming. God still could have carried it all, all my emotions and heartache and sadness of loss. Satan had me thinking on these things instead of fully trusting my Father, who is able to keep all that concerns me and protect me even emotionally.

Dr. Geraldo, a diabetic specialist, dear Christian friend, and brother, was right when he said the medicine would help me until I was able to help myself. Medication won't do much good unless you are able to work on what took you there in the first place. We stayed on the field for another year and a half, but in the end, my physical health was further hurt by the delay of not returning to the States to get the help I needed.

I had not taken anything for my nerves, and the anxiety remained where it was hard to leave the house. I attended the services and did what I could do in the work, but it took every effort and fiber of my being.

Diane and Russ Dean came to see us, and he gave me a book titled "Tell Yourself the Truth" by William Backus and Marie Chapman. It was a real help to me as the scriptures and changing my thought pattern helped me back to health. It wasn't easy; in fact, it was hard work to retrain my mind to rely on God—then, when accomplished, I found rest. Satan took advantage of my weak and fearful times.

Many times, it added to that fear tucked inside, and the ugly monster just grew. There was the famous cat burglar, Fernando da Gata, who kept us all in suspense. He had become famous for his terrorizing, entering homes and leaving proof that he was present, then sneaking out undetected while families were home. From one end of town to the other, heavily armed police patrolled the streets and highways for days. Nervous residents began buying guns.

One businessman was so taunted by a telephone call saying he was next that in hearing sounds in the middle of the night, he shot at a figure lingering in the dark. Fear took the life of his adolescent daughter with one shot. The call turned out to be a prank from an individual making light of what was happening with the cat burglar in the city of Pouso Alegre. The person just wanted to frighten him. Our hearts went out to this man as we, too, felt the fear for our families from this awful intruder. This businessman became mayor a few years later.

After two weeks, he was finally captured and killed. He was buried in the city cemetery, but because of protests from the townspeople, he was removed and buried elsewhere. No one wanted to remember the terror he put them through.

A few years before this event, I had faced another intruder twice, the first time as he was threatening our daughter April that he would hurt her if she said anything in the hallway of our home in town. I looked at him from the bedroom, threw the towels that I had just folded, and got in his face. I pushed him against the door, screaming in Portuguese that he was invading our home and not to dare touch my child. He moved, but I pushed him against the wall, and he grabbed the door handle and took off.

The second time he attempted to break in, I saw him in time opening the door. I then let him get his head inside and then slammed the door with his head caught between, hurting him so badly he stood dazed, which gave me plenty of time to lock the door. These things can happen anywhere, in the U.S., Brazil, or anywhere man resides. There is nothing new under the sun. I was still in love with the Brazilian people and our work among them.

Most recently, before my physical and emotional exhaustion hit, the mafia just happened to land on our doorstep in the middle of the night. Five criminals escaped, overturning their car, running from the police, and ended up hiding on our camp property.

Waiting for us to turn in, the criminals took the rugs from the front porch for padding on the soccer field bleachers until our porch lights were out. God had put us in a deep sleep as they tried to break in. Glass was shattered but had fallen onto the carpet, which made it difficult for us to hear it in the bedrooms; their attempt at prying the door open failed. The door was just a hair from opening for them. Frustrated, the thieves hotwired our car and took off. By the blood stains evident on the porch, one or more of the men had been shot.

The next morning, when I discovered what had partially taken place and the car was gone, I went up to the highway and flagged down a bus. The bus driver, familiar with us in the area, notified the police upon entering the city of Pouso Alegre. Bill stayed, gathering glass and calming the children. Soon, a few police arrived and filled in the blanks for us of what had taken place.

We did not realize the danger our family was in at the time, but when the police came and filled us in, we knew God had protected us through it all. One officer said that if they had succeeded in entering somehow or if we had opened the door, we would not have had a story to tell. The police were dealing with some very dangerous characters.

That situation was what made me fear the most. When an event hard to forget is played over and over in your mind, your body is drained of chemicals, such as serotonin, dopamine, etc., needed for the brain and emotions to function properly. We were without a phone at the camp

Still, Still Green Bananas

and had been without for 14 years and didn't mind, but 911 would have been great to have in times of emergency.

The safety we felt was, at best, questionable. One of our solutions was hooking up a car battery to an irritating horn that rang through the neighborhood. Our neighbors kept their rifles close by, if ever needed, after that event. We had wonderful neighbors, and we all would rally together if needed.

My trust in the Lord was overwhelmed by events and placed on the back burner, not realizing. Bill and I loved the Brazilian people, our church family, and the work God called us to do, but we forgot we are only human.

♦ ♦ ♦ ♦ ♦

Our children both attended Brazilian schools and loved it. Robert and April spoke Portuguese and English fluently. One day after school, while I was waiting to pick them up, a woman on staff approached me. "Your children might be in danger," she replied. "Dona Carol, please have you or your husband come early to pick up your children."

When I questioned the reason for this change, the school assistant replied, "The United States has just declared airstrikes against Libya, and many are afraid the U.S. is trying to start a third world war. For their safety, it might be good to pick them up earlier."

The United States bombing of Libya in 1986, code-named Operation El Dorado Canyon, comprised air strikes by the United States against Libya on April 15, 1986. Shortly after his inauguration in 1981, Libya was a strong priority for Ronald Reagan. Gaddafi was firmly anti-Israel. Many detailed reasons led to the attack. Fear ran through us at the thought she had introduced me to, but the Lord kept them safe.

Yes, missionaries can be in danger because of the decisions the United States makes. Pray for your missionaries. My prayer is that God blesses and protects each one who lifts up the name of Jesus.

Not too long after this incident, we realized if April wanted to go to college, then we were going to have to do something about her English. At this point, April is 14, and she introduces us to the Pan American

Christian Academy in the city of São Paulo, originally started for missionary children. At first, it was a flat no; I wouldn't think of it! Then, visiting the campus, she really wanted to go. From eighth grade through her senior year, she studied and prepared for college while living with two wonderful families across the street from P.A.C.A. Even though we tried to get to most of her activities, we felt we were missing out on so much of her life.

The school was only four hours away, but for us, it would be 16 if we picked her up and took her home for the weekend. Four hours to go to pick her up, four back, stay a night or two, back in the car to take her to Monday classes early, and then the drive back for Bill, Robert, and me. For a pastor busy on the weekends with church activities, it finally took a toll. We began once a month to bring her home, and once a month, we went to spend time with her; it was easier on everyone.

April is a people person. She had to be around other students, classmates, and friends; it was her friends that helped motivate her as well as some very special teachers. So, going to P.A.C.A. made her blossom into a talented young lady. There were difficulties and homesickness she felt, and guilt I felt as a mother for not being there when she was going through hard times. Satan would use those times to further beat me down. She developed musically and educationally, and we were proud of her accomplishments.

Robert, five years younger, went to a Brazilian school until he was in the fifth grade when we started homeschooling so he wouldn't end up in the same situation as April with her English. Class was every day from 8:00 to noon, and we were very consistent. Then we all had lunch, and the afternoon was to be spent on homework, visiting, marketing, and baking, etc. Robert was pretty self-motivated with just a little push here and there, so class time was enjoyable. It was funny, however, when he asked if he could fast-forward his teacher since we were doing ABEKA video studies. Clever! There are some classes and teachers I have wanted to fast forward too! Robert went through 9th grade in the States and then went to P.A.C.A. also, for 10th grade. He then graduated from Hillcrest High School in Springfield, Missouri. Both of our children fit into the Brazilian culture very well and loved it, but we wanted them also to remember their U.S. heritage.

◆ ◆ ◆ ◆ ◆

Many of our Brazilian family and friends were killed on the highways of Brazil, one right after another. One year was especially hard. In trying to be strong for them and their families, since they have to be buried within 24 hours, I found I didn't take the time needed to grieve myself. I began to fear for our family's safety as well. Sadness, grief, fear of failing my children, self-disappointments, and worry began to dominate my every thought, not the mercy, trust, and promises of God.

In the end, it wasn't the mafia, a cat burglar, or accidents on the highway that took me out of our ministry in Brazil; it was the buildup of fear of what if or what might happen that did it. The fear of those things happening became just as real as if the events took place a second time. Satan likes to keep us there, feeling paralyzed.

I thought I was surrendered; here I was, a missionary, and I loved the Lord. Stress and worry were the biggest obstacles in the way of God doing what He wanted to do in my life. I became an obsessive worrier, and the way out was going to be long and difficult but not impossible.

> *"Nay but, O man, who art thou that repliest against God? Shall the thing formed say to him that formed it, Why hast thou made me thus?"* **Romans 9:20**

I was telling God He made a mistake. Who am I to tell God He didn't know what He was doing?

Still, Still Green Bananas

CHAPTER FOUR:
AT PEACE OR IN PIECES

Still, Still Green Bananas

I really wanted to tell God He had done something wrong when I hit rock bottom in 1990. Bill was by my side every day, reading the Word and reminding me of how much God loved me. I knew that, but was understanding of things was blurred by my emotions and chemical deficit that took place. I listened to Bud McCord's tapes and studies of the New Testament at the time. If God doesn't condemn me, why do I condemn myself?

For the first three months of this situational depression, the lack of serotonin, etc., made me think things I had never dreamed I would think. A mental warfare was on, and God was fighting it for me because I had no strength of my own. I gave it all to Him because I was tired and exhausted, and God told me to rest in Him, and I laid back and let Him do a refining work in me.

Satan tried to convince me that God had abandoned me and that it was not worth living. He whispered it would be better for everyone if I just took my life or just gave up. He continued to whisper, "Here you are, a missionary, and where is your God now? You've given up so much. Where'd it get you? I had actually given nothing. You must have failed big time for Him to abandon you like this.

Even in the darkest part, I knew the truth, but trying to sort through it all at the time was sort of like walking through murky water, slow motion, and heavy feet— cloudy at best. My heart condemned me, but the scripture told me in John 3:19-24 that God is greater than our hearts. My heart had lied to me. There was a long way to go, and Hand in hand with the Lord, we took it together. Bill walked with me, and God held us both, leaving only one footprint: His.

> *For though we walk in the flesh, we do not war after the flesh: for the weapons of our warfare are not carnal, but mighty through God to the pulling down of strongholds; casting down the imaginations, and every high thing that exalteth itself against the knowledge of God, and bringing into captivity every thought to the obedience of Christ." 2nd Corinthians 10:3-5*

I would fight back but not in a physical way because I had no strength of my own. I began to cling to the scripture like never before. In Psalms, You are my rock and my salvation; only in thee will I trust. I saw Satan trying to ruin another pastor's wife in the same city—Satan was angry and began to do a heavy job on the wives. I clung to Jesus with all my strength and might, but—thank goodness it was He who was hanging on to me.

I pictured myself always in a tug-of-war with Satan, pulling and tugging trying to stay away and eaten up by his deceit. But one day in Brazil, while studying for my junior class, I began trying to explain to the children how he works. I then realized a better way to see the dilemma.

We are positioned in Christ if we have asked Him for forgiveness of sins and asked Him to reign in our hearts. Not...

Satan_____Me_____God
            (Not little ole me in tug of war)

Better seen as described below!

I am at God's right hand at the top of the totem pole, and Satan is at the bottom—what better place to be, huh? Picture up and down—not across in the tug-of-war—God's power is great!

Where is Satan in all this? He is at the bottom of the totem pole, while we are at the right hand of God. What a better perspective, don't you think? Satan is nothing, will be nothing, and has no power over us unless we allow him to. I don't feel so tired now in my thinking—I just let God take care of him—after all, the battle is between God and Satan, and we know who will win. All I do is rest in Him—most of the time, when I don't try to take him on in my own power.

Sometimes, I forget and begin to wrestle with fear and then go back to the drawing board of the basics to remember my position in Christ. Jill Briscoe is one of the most influential writers to me. Many years ago, I was inspired by her hooking me into what she wanted her readers to understand and grasp. How to Follow the Shepherd (when the sheep keep pushing you around) is by far my favorite book. I have read it numerous times. Her words penned on paper, encouraged by the Lord to tell her story, led me, I believe, into writing my story.

Jill pointed out this verse in Psalm 56:8, "Thou tallest my wanderings: put thou my tears into thy bottle: are they not in thy book?" How wonderful to know those tearful times are just as important to God as those praises lifted to Him. Even my tearful times were written down. How personal! Psalm 139:16 also reveals how much God cares.

"Thine eyes did see my substance, yet being imperfect; and in thy book all my members were written, which in continuance were fashioned, when as yet there was none of them." Even my members, my substance, including my chemical makeup such as neurotransmitters to the brain serotonin and dopamine were known. That is personal and exciting. God understands that which He created.

I didn't understand until 18 months later, when I came back to the U.S., what all I had suffered from was the stress on my body. At this time, I learned a lot about myself. I had chosen to tough it out, thinking what I was experiencing would all go away, like waking up the next morning as if nothing had happened to me. Didn't happen! Bill and I were very much in love with the congregation we were working in, and souls were being saved despite the slow healing process. Our brother and sister Brazilians wrapped their warm and loving arms around us and nurtured us as family.

Bill was the most wonderful mate and loving companion as always encouraging every step of the journey, even if he didn't quite understand it all. I was sent tapes of Bud McCord's messages and listened to them whenever possible, trying to put everything in God's perspective. He spoke f 1 Peter 5:10 But the God of all grace who hath called us unto his eternal glory by Christ Jesus, after that ye have suffered a while, make you perfect, stablish, strengthen, settle you. Bud McCord described perfect in this verse as mature, stable in Christ, using His power not your own, and not easily frightened. That last one is easier said than done.

Chemical deficits occur when the body's normal amount of chemicals needed for the brain, diminishes under stress, illness, worry, or trauma. Just as a diabetic, his body does not supply enough insulin so must we need supplements. Some diabetics don't watch their diet and have serious complications, while others do everything right, and the pancreas or liver just gives out. So as with the chemicals in the brain; sometimes we just need some help to replenish the supply and get back to a healthy life, and we must see what causes the stress and do something about it. Also, we must stay in the Word of God. He must be allowed to help us soul search.

My thoughts and thought patterns have changed tremendously changing to what God thinks of me not what others think of me. Healing from any physical or emotional wound takes time. I desperately wanted a shortcut through this process crying "Get me out of this Lord, please!" Even Bill wished it to be gone, but my body had experienced tremendous stress and now we needed more than ever to trust in our sovereign God. God is faithful He would see us through and there would be a rainbow on the other side.

The power that saved me was going to keep me, even though Satan was not going to let up. He tempted me for three months to take my life---but I confessed this to Bill, and He stayed on his knees by my bed, reminding me of God's truth and his promises, reading with me scripture as my meals literally. I was not hungry, and I lost 20 lbs. quickly. He reminded me God does not abandon his own. Finally, I began to gather strength. I could see light at the end of the tunnel.

God created this very important part of us called our emotions and they are more delicate than we know. We must have a good emotional as well as spiritual balance. Fear stunted my growth. Fears such as fear of failure, fear of acceptance, or fear of not being loved etc. These fears control us if we let them.

> *For God hath not given us the spirit of fear; but of power and of love and of a sound mind. 2 Timothy 1:7*

or

> *There is no fear in love; but perfect love casteth out fear; because fear hath torment. He that feareth is not made perfect in love.*
> *1 John 4:18*

Fearing that something might happen takes just as much out of us as if the thing you feared really happened. That is something to think about. I gave myself no room for mistakes and placed too high expectations on myself—unreachable and unrealistic. Jill Briscoe wrote, "Failure is to be expected, but failure is not final." Most things we rate as big are really nothing at all. Have you heard the expression making a mountain out of a molehill? It is not the end of the world if the food you buy through the drive-thru is cold or the car breaks down. We need to put everything in the right perspective. Yes, if someone in your family received news he or she has cancer, that is big, not whether or not you couldn't buy the right shade of nail polish.

I must confront new situations daily to see whether I am growing or not or whether fear or sin has stunted my growth. God will not kick you while you are down, but he will give you his hand and lift you up if you accept it. He will allow you to try again.

I bore you on eagles wings, and brought you unto myself.
Exodus 19:4

How beautiful! How precious also are thy thoughts unto me, O
God! How great is the sum of them! Search me, O God, and
know my heart: try me, and know my thoughts: and see if there be
any wicked way in me, and lead me in the way everlasting.
Psalm 139:17, 23-24.

Still, Still Green Bananas

CHAPTER FIVE: NO SHORTCUTS

Still, Still Green Bananas

Israelite history has always fascinated me. We can criticize the children of Israel for their behavior, but in actuality, I don't believe we would have acted much differently by what I see in human nature and culture around me. Of course, I am not called upon to walk through a desert leaving Egypt behind, walk through the Red Sea, live in tents, or almost die of thirst. I am, however, to learn from their example, whether good or bad.

How would we have faced the Red Sea? I can see the panic attack now as I look at roaring walls of water on either side. Even Bill, my husband, fearless in most situations, would need to be tied and blindfolded to get him through because of his fear of water. I think it has to do with a canoe trip in 1974 while on staff at Cherry St. Baptist Church. I know I would tremble in my sandals, frozen to the spot, while my insides shake like maracas.

Finally, I would move swiftly to the other side, afraid all the while. Someone would yell, "Hurry up, the enemy is coming! Get out of my way. I'm coming through." In their panic, they would trample over others, missing the great miracle before them. Isn't that just like us to miss what God wanted us to see? The doubtful ones would go ahead, not fully believing those walls of water would not collapse. The faithful would stick to their marching orders, believing that their guide who took them out of Egypt would see them through to the Promised Land.

If we know Christ as our Savior, we are bound for the other side, but oh, how much easier it would be if we could fully entrust our situations and circumstances to the Lord's hands. Then we could respect, not fear, the roaring of the waves. I remember when Robert asked Jesus into his heart. We were on our way to the city from the camp and were talking about his Sunday school lesson. Robert said, "Well, Mom, if God can part the Red Sea, then He can save me and give me a place in heaven, can't He?" I stopped the car by the side of the road, and there, at seven years of age, Robert asked Jesus into his heart. If only I could perceive all God wants me to know through His word! A young boy knew.

Robert understood about the grace of God, but spiritual maturity would be a lot to expect at his age. One day I was cleaning the kitchen when I saw Robert pass through the dining room with the children's devotional book. I felt so proud and puffed up inside thinking, "That is our son!" I wanted to believe he understood what daily Bible study meant. I remembered thinking, "Boy, he's really taking his newfound faith in the Lord seriously."

Realizing how quiet it had become, I began my search for him. I opened the front door, but he was nowhere to be found. Then, I viewed the devotional book neatly placed on top of a mayonnaise jar full of worms. Needless to say, he had not been reading the devotional book; I was sure to letdown. Talk about unrealistic expectations! He was covering the worms so they would not get away and had gone to get more. Now that is realistic behavior for a seven-year-old.

There are no shortcuts. We all must grow up...going through the stages of a 7, 11, 15, or 17-year-old, all a part of the maturing process. We don't jump from seven-year-old thinking to 47-year-old understanding, although some may mature a little faster than others. There may be some forced to mature sooner because of certain experiences, but most will have to go through the typical maturing steps until the emotional and physical aspects catch up with each other.

We must have realistic goals for our children. Just because they are saved does not mean they won't go through the aches and pains of pre-adolescence, teen, or early adulthood. As we have all seen, some children will mature faster than others, but still, kids will be kids. As a parent, I had no magic potion for growing up kids. They just had to go through life's experiences. They had their nasty, ornery, obstinate days, just as anyone else. So did their mother. So why would I expect more out of them than I did of myself?

When my sister Beverly and I were young, we would cut through the woods to get to school instead of walking the block or two around to the front of the school. One day we glanced down beside the path and there lay someone with very small feet. We took off running, screaming and yelling that there was a midget lying dead in the woods. There was someone, not a midget maybe, but Beverly and I felt that outsider invaded our space.

My sister and I did not quite trust our often-used shortcut after that as we imagined someone lying in the weeds waiting to jump out at us. At that time, the children's stories of trolls and the goats crossing over the bridge were very big. I was very vulnerable, and those things frightened me. Maybe that's why, as kids, we did not like the huge Mackinaw Bridge going to Sault Ste. Marie in the Upper Peninsula of Michigan.

How many times I have come close to fainting when I wished there was a shortcut to avoid the turmoil and suffering; but life is not like that. In those difficult-to-trust times, we see that the Lord does bring us through. Resting is so much easier than kicking and fighting. Why are some lessons so hard for us to learn?

Shortcuts are not always the best. Sooner or later, that time may be spent doing and redoing, making up time you thought you had saved. For some things, there just are no shortcuts. Going through the whole process may be a very necessary task to be the person God wants you to be. Taking shortcuts is asking for a delay in God's plan for your life. Things we are learning now could have been learned already and maybe a little less painfully.

If you desire and demand to take shortcuts, God will not stand in your way, and just as with me, you may take a few wrong turns or shortcuts in the process. But as Psalm 56:13 reads:

> *"For thou hast delivered my soul from death: wilt not thou deliver my feet from falling, that I may walk before God in the light of the living?"*

He will keep me from falling. It is a promise!

Still, Still Green Bananas

CHAPTER SIX: PRESSURE PAN DILEMMA

Still, Still Green Bananas

Still, Still Green Bananas

Christmas of 1975, just a few days before Bill, April, and I left for Brazil, we exchanged gifts as usual. I anxiously and curiously opened my gift to find an electric pressure pan, a new item then that is hard to find today. Boy, was I disappointed? A pressure pan; what would I do with it? I was scared to death of these pans. I could see it now, the lid exploding, food all over the ceiling, and who knows where they would find my body parts.

Little did I know what a blessing that pressure pan would be on the field; with everything fresh all year round, there was no need for many canned foods. I had no canned green beans, beans, pumpkin, etc., to open just whenever I needed them. Beans and rice were a daily part of our meals, and I needed to cook them two or three times a week. I finally acted delighted with my Christmas present after I stopped murmuring under my breath.

When working with a pressure pan, you must watch the temperature, not put too much food in the pan, and certainly have enough liquid. Experience is the best teacher. Thank the good Lord He gave me the courage to venture out and try this new addition to my kitchen "use-tensils." I decided not to pack it in the back of the cupboard like I had forgotten all about it. It became part of my necessary equipment for surviving in new surroundings. I still own a pressure pan and love using it often.

Like the pressure pan, we build up inside a normal defense that can stand pressure for a certain length of time according to each individual's stress limit. Just as cooking time varies with each food, we can all withstand varying amounts of pressure, but too much can be disastrous or cause us to lose control. We need to know boundaries, limits, and when to put on the brakes before we break. Bitterness, irritability, depression, impatience, unhappiness, negative thoughts, and low self-esteem are symptoms of a pressure overload.

I remember wanting to understand how some could read the very same verse from the Bible and get so much more out of it than me. Then I realized that some of the greatest authors of our devotional books, sermons, and commentaries could not have completely understood the meaning without first having been tested and tried themselves. I wanted to see deeper into the Scriptures myself as Paul did. I pleaded with the Lord that I could be more devoted to Him than just habitual Scripture reading. Little did I know that a purification of the very remotest corners of my heart would have to take place. The pressure was on. God wanted a better relationship with me to develop me more for His purpose.

When the pressure pan exploded, I was still picking up the pieces weeks and months later. Some people would say that God allowed me to go through this experience to help others who had similar experiences. But at that time, I could hardly help myself. I see things differently now, but then something else had to take place first.

People react to stress or tension in different ways. Some may develop ulcers, the buildup of acids under continual stress, and bad eating habits because that is where they are most sensitive. Some have severe migraines and heaviness in the chest. Headaches may begin with tremendous hormonal fluctuations.

My good doctor helped me to discover what was causing the continual pain and pressure. Bill knew I was not inventing this pain as he helped me through many times of suffering. I massaged my chest muscles when the pain worsened after some exercise, lifting, or coughing. My doctor diagnosed this condition as Costochondritis, a condition caused by trauma to the chest, which causes painful inflammation. This trauma may be anxiety or an actual blow to the chest. I had gone 1 ½ years with nothing to calm my anxiety after the breakdown. This caused severe anxiety, where I could not leave the house and was physically frightened easily.

Before the condition was properly diagnosed, I believed I would never find an answer, so I lived with the pain. It was not a continual panic attack, but it was an inflammation that would flare with activity or tension. When I began to feel tense in that area, I learned to relax, breathe deeply, and think through what was causing the anxiety, reminding myself that nothing is too big for God. I have not felt the pain for many years; there was a simple cure of an anti-inflammatory. If only I had known earlier. What a relief.

My medical knowledge is limited, and I have tried to explain this as best I can; please do not try to diagnose yourself. If you are experiencing discomfort in this area, please talk to your doctor. I'm just beginning to understand how my system works and reacts. My prayer is that you will also.

As I listened to the radio recently, I heard Charles Stanley say the main purpose of trials is purification. I am to develop and change my attitudes and habits, which are also sins if not controlled by God—maybe not like in open rebellion, but still sin. God gets our attention by allowing these attitudes and wrong responses to surface. Now, I love Him even more because that shows me how personal a God He is. He must work in me first; then, if He chooses to let me help someone else, I will gladly do so and accept that ministry.

In some cases, we can only help so much. Then, those most troubled need qualified counseling. It took everything I had to admit that I needed help through this trial. When the pressure built and exploded for everyone to see, I knew I had to swallow my pride and get help. Dr. States Skipper of Springfield, Missouri, helped me, and I then went to the Minirth-Meier Clinic, going to classes for three weeks. My motel was only a couple of blocks away, and the walk was refreshing.

Wise Christian counselors guided me; I did the working through, and God did the healing. I wanted to understand how I ended up where I did. Now, I have learned tools to help me see when the pressure is on and when to back it off. I know, without a doubt, God's unconditional love for me. What happened to me is called a "Situational Depression," where stress and situations beyond our control sometimes bring about the pressure pan dilemma. Like the mafia hitting our house, close calls on the highway, boarding school for the children, etc.

I thank Him daily for His healing power, and He can do the same for you. Satan still tries to get a foothold on me, but I am seated on high with Christ at the right hand of God. What power we have in Christ! I knew about that power and had exercised it many times over, but these times seemed tougher, and false guilt led me to believe lies.

Yes, Satan will continue to put pressure on those full noble spots, but we must not give him room to operate. We have power through Christ. Philippians 4:13. There will be pressures, but remember one day the heat will be turned up on old Satan, Lucifer himself, and no longer will we feel the heat of his temptations and pain from his trickery.

I was a missionary, so how could I have allowed the pressure to build in such a way? Why have so many great preachers fallen and preachers' wives become emotionally wrecked and burned out? We sin when we put ourselves in a place where we feel Satan cannot touch us anymore. As I said, one day we will not feel the heat of his temptations and the pain from his trickery, but that is not now; Satan has not been defeated yet. We must continually be alert until the day of our Lord's appearing.

Inside I was facing those built-up fears head-on. Apprehension is the same as fear. The fear of something happening can cause the same stress on our bodies as if something actually happened. The fear drains us of serotonin, a much-needed neurotransmitter. When a similar situation arises, a subconscious button is pushed, and apprehension turns to exaggerated fear. That is imagination running away with itself. We limit sin to things such as murder, robbery, and drinking. Sin is sin—worrying, backbiting, false witness against another, and swearing, etc.

Paul is saying that there is much more to the Christian life and God, and God, being a very personal God, wanted me to experience that. Philippians 4:8 tells me I am to think on things that are true, honest, pure, and just. He did not list all the things we should or should not do in this verse, but what we should think. If we do not think as this verse says, then we are sinning against God. That is where I failed big time with my thoughts and fears. I gave my thoughts and emotions completely over to fear—replacing my trust and faith in God Almighty.

Do not be afraid to let the light of the Word reveal the innermost part of you. Read Psalm 119:11, Philippians 1:6, 2 Corinthians 4:16, "renewed," 1 Corinthians 4:21, and allow Him to come in the spirit of meekness, not with a rod. Let God turn down the heat to calm and steady. If you want to blow your lid, go ahead or just act like you have it all together. Storms may come, and some may reveal things about us that we otherwise would not have discovered.

CHAPTER SEVEN: YOUR WAY OR MINE

Still, Still Green Bananas

Bill and I had the necessary book knowledge about ministry but not much practical experience when we arrived in Brazil. How would the methods we learned work here? How would I learn how to prepare new foods and new ways of doing things? I sure thought I missed my American mop, can opener, and American products I was used to.

Determined, I quickly learned how to fix fresh green beans, chop my own chocolate pieces for chocolate chips, and make my own maple syrup, pancakes, biscuits, etc., all from scratch. It was fun. I traded my mop for a bucket of water, a squeegee, and a big rag to wash the ceramic tiles that were soaked with water and cleaning solution, then dried with a big rag wrapped on the squeegee. I now miss "everything Brazilian." How funny we are.

Learning Portuguese at the language school took a lot of time, so once a week, a young lady would help me clean with a 4-year-old and a new one on the way. I was not used to not having hot running water, but we kept boiling it on the stove. I tried very desperately to communicate with the young lady. She came early one day and asked for bread to eat. I misunderstood and gave her a rag, directing her where to start cleaning. Oops! She was hungry, and I gave her rags.

Then, one day, soon after Robert was born, I asked my young helper to clean my stove and help me with the diapers. Later, I looked in the kitchen to find my stove was missing, and the pail of soaked diapers was gone. In amazement, I looked outside and saw the stove being hosed down and shining beautifully in the backyard. The diapers were neatly laid out all over the lawn, bleaching in the sun. Robert had the best, whitest diapers around.

◆◆◆◆◆

The language was difficult in the beginning, and we made a lot of mistakes. Not too long after starting language school, I answered a knock at the front door. I opened the little security window to see four men with brooms in their hands, jabbering to me in Portuguese. Not understanding a word but thinking they were selling brooms, I politely said, "Hoje não," the very two words we were told to say if someone was begging or selling something. Well, I said, "Hoje não" or "not today," and went about my work.

The next day, I saw these very same men again, but this time, they were in the park across the street, and they still had those same brooms. They watched us like hawks and were not very pleasant at all by their expressions. For the next couple of days, as we would go in and out of the house, they were always there in the park and treated us in a cool manner. Bill and I realized the men were gardeners. I was dumbfounded and wanted to know why they treated us so. The next day, I asked one of our more experienced missionaries, Dave Howell, to go over and ask what the problem seemed to be.

We knew everything was all right since he was almost rolling on the ground in laughter. He explained that these gardeners had asked me if they could use our porch for a few minutes to stand under since it had started to rain. I was only saying what I was told to say, my two words, "not today," and refused them shelter from the rain. After the men understood, they received us with thumbs-up and big smiles, showing they had no more hurt feelings and even had a good laugh.

By the way, the men were not selling brooms; they were hand trimming around plants and bushes with scissors and hedge clippers. The brooms were used to sweep off sidewalks and even break up the cut grass. These men were hard workers and very forgiving people once they understood my predicament. It was quite hilarious afterward but, at the time, a bit humbling.

A few weeks later, I dared to go get some coconut ice cream and practiced the words all the way across and down the street. I reached the corner store, practicing one last time before entering. There was one problem. I could not remember which word I should use. The same word could change the whole meaning if the accent was placed on the wrong syllable: "Co'co" or "Coco'." I needed to say the word with the accent on the first "o."

Needless to say, I said it wrong and asked the man for some bowel movement flavored ice cream instead of coconut flavored. How embarrassing! I left without my ice cream. When I told Bill what happened, he said, "They must have been out of that flavor today—you can go back tomorrow." Not me! I'll never go back to that place, and I haven't!

Portuguese words all sounded the same to us in the beginning, but one accent can change the whole meaning of the word, just as one flaw can harm our Christian character and change the meaning of Christ-like. Practice being Christ-like and I am sure you will do a better job than I did at getting it right.

◆◆◆◆◆

After living in Campinas for two years and taking a short furlough, we found ourselves moving to Pouso Alegre in the state of Minas Gerais. Opening a new work had challenges of its own, but the fresh paint and newly built pews gave us more incentive than ever. Visits and tracts were handed out, and the first Sunday was certainly bathed in prayer.

The painter came to the house before doing the work on the church. As he approached the house, he knocked and I opened the front door. He politely asked if my dad was home. I was around 28 years of age and Bill was about to turn 30. Since Bill's hair had grayed early, people always guessed him at 45 to 50. We had a lot of fun with that, or at least I did.

When the man asked if my dad was home, I just could not resist saying loud enough for Bill to hear, "Yes, I will go get my daddy." By that time, Bill had come from behind the door with his hand in the form of a fist, asking me with a grin if I wanted to swallow it. I laughed even more.

Out of embarrassment, the painter came to our first church services. He and his little girl were present with Bill, April, Robert, and me. That was a big crowd for the first Sunday service in Pouso Alegre. Many times no one came to services, so after waiting for an hour or so, we would close the doors, go home, and tearfully ask God to provide someone to hear His Word besides our own family. Sure, one-year-old Robert and 6-year-old April were pretty tired of being preached to.

Bill and I had made so many visits and drank so much strong coffee we stared at the ceiling at night unable to sleep. This went on for four months, then God's blessings broke loose. What if we had given up? Praise the Lord for His strength to follow through.

Our time in Brazil taught us some of life's most valuable lessons. Many of their ways were different for me, but I learned to prefer many of them. Their way was different and interesting but not wrong. It was right for them and their culture.

Now, if someone passes by my house and sees laundry all over the yard, they will understand. If it is neatly folded, it is a garage sale. If each piece is spread out on the lawn and normally white in color, then I am bleaching. If my husband is on the lawn, it is because he is bleached out, and I am trying to get his Brazilian tan back.

Our way is not always God's way. Isaiah 55:8 says,

"For my thoughts are not your thoughts, neither are your ways my ways, saith the Lord."

We need to learn how to recognize God's ways. They may seem strange at first, but they are far better for us. He is a wise Father; He will not mislead us.

"Be still, and know that I am God." Psalm 46:10

In other words, be still, listen, and if you study the Word, you will easily recognize if it be of God. He has everything under control. God's bidding will become easier to acknowledge when we practice His ways.

CHAPTER EIGHT:
LIFE IS FULL OF SURPRISES

Still, Still Green Bananas

Our family had only been in Brazil for two weeks when our daughter April became disturbingly ill. At 3 1/2 years of age, she was curled up in a ball, and we couldn't get her to stretch out and relax her body. It was as if she were a yo-yo all rolled up and strung tight. At 2 o'clock in the morning, we were desperate; there was no telephone, and we knew no Portuguese. A fellow missionary lived in the big city of Campinas, so we wrote his address down on a piece of paper. Bill then went out to flag down a taxi, handing him the address of the missionary. We arrived at 4 AM at the Simpsons' home and stayed there until we could get in to see a doctor.

We were told that April had some severe allergy problems causing asthma with muscle spasms in her chest, causing her to double up. Little did we know that we had placed her close to mold or mildew. To our naked eye, we could not see what was forming behind the paint on the wall where April slept. I had carefully placed mats and blankets on the floor with Bill, myself, and April against the wall where she would feel me on one side and the wall on the other. Our bedroom furniture had not yet arrived by ship, so we would be camping on the floor for two to three months.

April's little body had a reaction to the mold covered up by a good paint job. We did move her to the center of the room, but she still had difficulty. A little at a time, it became greener, fuzzier, and nastier. Needless to say, we were glad when the beds arrived and we could get her off the floor and away from the walls. The doctor suggested we move to a drier climate like Brasilia, but God had other plans.

Many rough days, months, and years were ahead for April; some days were great, others difficult to get through. Sometimes, she was assaulted by a horrendous cough, causing painful spasms in her chest. Bill and I would have to hold her for up to 30 hours at a time, taking turns. I would sometimes need to massage her muscles to help calm the spasms, like a bad Charlie horse, as she described later. Any cold virus or infection became difficult for her.

When April was a little older, tests were done in Ann Arbor, Michigan, showing scar tissue from all the difficulties she had suffered. By the time she was 13, the attacks had become less frequent—maybe once or twice a month rather than daily—all with the help of an inhalation machine, medication, and her own body maturing. Difficulties still plague her as an adult, but pneumonia shots have cut down visits to the hospital.

In November 1977, Robert was a month old, and April had just turned five in June. We wanted April to accept her new baby brother into her world, but now Mom and Dad's attention would be divided with this new addition. Up till now, she loved having him, but time would tell if he was worth keeping, as a brother and sister would consider. We all decided to take a trip to the little tourist town, Serra Negra, known for knitted and crocheted baby clothes, so she could pick out an outfit or two for Robert.

Little did we know that day would be so adventurous. We started our hour-long drive with perfect weather for the trip. We built this day up to April so she would be really excited. I packed a lot of diapers, munchies, and even a pair of slacks to change into. I had always wanted to ride up the mountain on the chairlift, but I figured today was not the day with a newborn.

When we arrived in Serra Negra, we found the public bathrooms in the little park. I was feeling a bit queasy from the drive but didn't think a whole lot about it. When I was walking to the restroom, I began to feel worse. Bill became worried after I had been in there for some time. He had not heard me call him, and no one else was around.

I was hemorrhaging.

I began to panic a bit, then realized I had to figure this out on my own. Thank goodness I had taken my bag with me, which is a habit mothers do with young children. I took my skirt off and changed into my slacks; they would help secure more padding until I could get to the car. The padding consisted of Robert's cloth diapers and my skirt. Near passing out, I struggled to get to the car when Bill came to my rescue, asking a thousand questions that I myself could not answer.

Bill helped me into the back seat to lie down and strapped 5-year-old April in the front seat of our light blue Volkswagen. I held Robert close to me, and I'm sure he knew something was not right, but he seemed to be calmer than me. We felt the best thing to do was to try to get back to the city of Campinas, where everything was more familiar and, of course, where my doctor was.

With no time to waste, Bill took off around the mountains and headed for home. We stopped at the house for more supplies for Robert before heading to the hospital, and I decided to change clothes. I lost so much more blood that I became frightened. We dropped the baby, April, and a bag of supplies off at Larry and Sharon Haggs' home, dear BBF missionary friends. But there was one thing: I could not leave my milk. Our son was breastfeeding, and he would need supper soon, or the whole of Campinas would hear.

I cried all the way to the hospital, concerned about our month-old baby boy eating. I was so disturbed about our baby not being with me that the nurses made Bill promise me he would get him so I could nurse. I had been examined and was asleep when Bill arrived with Robert. He later told me how funny it was to have Robert breastfeeding and me out like a light. The nurse was helpful in holding Robert to make sure he was fed. I was on my side, and Robert was tucked beside me, not even realizing what was going on.

He was hungry; he didn't care, although Sharon had intelligently fed him with a brand-new rubber glove, sterilizing it and putting a pinhole in one finger that was filled with milk. She was not about to let him go hungry. I will never forget that ingenuity.

The doctor explained why, after Robert's birth, breastfeeding was so painful for me and why I cried through every feeding. The doctor explained that a large portion of the placenta was still there after childbirth. This doctor said that she did not know why I didn't have gangrene and that the pain of breastfeeding should have been looked at. I was soon better and sent home to rest, while Robert never missed a meal. What an experience!

◆◆◆◆◆

Michigan in the fall of 1985 was beautiful, hearing crisp leaves crackle with every step as we shuffled through them. This was the time for cider and doughnuts. We loved visiting churches in Michigan in the fall, but it would be different at Pastor Art Kidd's Missions Conference. Just before the conference began, we visited my father-in-law in Ann Arbor, Michigan, at his senior citizen's apartment.

Still, Still Green Bananas

Since there was not enough room for all four of us, Bill and Robert drove over to his sister's house to spend the night. April and I spent the night at Dad Levergood's place. Dad Levergood had just enough room for April and me to sleep together in his bedroom while he slept on the couch.

While at Dad's, I began to feel irritation and swelling in my eyes, which I believed to be an allergic reaction to something in the air. I asked Dad if he had any Murine or eye drops for allergies. He then began to tell me about some eye drops in the bathroom cabinet. I found what he had described and proceeded to douse my eyes with those drops. It felt so good that I wasn't concerned with the amount I was using.

April and I turned in early, tired from the long trip, and at 8 o'clock the next morning, I awoke expecting to see a bright, sunny fall day. To my surprise, I opened my eyes to darkness. Frightened, I batted my eyelids a few more times but to no avail; I could not see. I was blind!

Panic struck me as I tried to wake April so she could call her daddy for me. We tried to be very quiet so as not to alarm Dad out on the couch. April dialed the number she found in my purse and called her Aunt Sandy. All of us tried to be very calm, but we were afraid, not knowing what I had put in my eyes. April read off the letters that made up the names of the drops I had used, and her aunt Sandy called the hospital. Within a short time, I learned that my eyes were dilated completely from an overdose of cataract medicine from Dad's surgery last year. Within ten days, I had my eyesight back.

The conference was sure interesting, having to wear my sunglasses and stumble around as I went up to the platform to give my testimony, but we survived. Of course, Bill took advantage of every situation possible, like reading strange things off the menu for me at the restaurant. I knew better than to believe Bill Levergood. I didn't know what to believe when he said my hair looked great; I just had to take his word for it.

The experience, once I knew what happened, was bearable, but the moment I opened my eyes to blindness, I was frightened. I had taken my eyesight for granted. Yes, life is full of surprises. Bill said he was getting a sign to put on the side of the car for when I drive, "Watch out, a blind woman is driving this car!" Ha ha! Funny, funny!

All of us expect to face normal days, but sometimes it just does not happen quite the way we expected. Some things we face are earthshaking, while others are normal, irritating, and even silly, making our days more interesting, like when I was brushing my teeth after returning from a trip. I had no time to drop my luggage off, so I ran into the dentist's office with my toothpaste.

I asked if I could use the restroom and, in a hurry, started brushing my teeth when I realized I had grabbed the wrong tube. I grabbed Deep Heat instead of Crest toothpaste. Now, that was some hot flash! My dentist got such a kick out of it that he still tells the story. That day, he teased me that I would not even need an anesthetic after using Deep Heat. Even my sinuses were cleared. That was one time my flossing made the situation worse. I'm just glad I made their day.

Growing up, I was protected under the umbrella of my home, my parents, my church, and people that loved me. That was an umbrella God used for my good. That did not mean there would not be difficult times in which I would not understand. As I matured, I saw life could be difficult; life is not always full of sunny days.

We do not have answers to some questions, and easy answers are not always correct. This is where our full trust in the Lord must be evident; we cannot know the mind of God, but we are to trust Him. If I can trust Him for eternal life, why then can I not trust any situation or circumstance into His hands? He is God, and I am to trust Him. Isaiah 41:10. Every day holds great opportunities, and each morning is a new day. I look forward to anticipating great things from God. This hope is the source of our strength and endurance.

◆ ◆ ◆ ◆ ◆

Beth Adams and I drove to our home state of Michigan together to see family and friends. Beth has been a very dear friend for many years, a friendship that began at Wick Rd., Baptist Church in Taylor, Michigan, in 1971 in our youth group. Dropping Beth off in Melvindale, Michigan to visit with her mother and sister, I proceeded to Flint to see Rachel Mooney, one of my dearest friends who was dying of cancer, which took me through Detroit.

This would be a new experience, even though I was familiar with Detroit as a passenger, never as a driver. Here I was, sandwiched between two bread trucks heading for their daily deliveries. Scared stiff, I held tightly to the steering wheel, held my breath, and plowed through. I remembered stories Bill told me of his delivering bread on his truck route throughout the town of Detroit in the summer of 1969. I wished he had been there with me.

I do not remember people being as friendly in Michigan as when on this trip. By my lonesome, I headed through the heaviest of traffic, driving Brazilian style—offensively. One lady went by with both hands waving in the air; friendly lady, I thought. But in reality, I knew she saw my license plate and probably had some choice words for this Missouri driver. I continued to drive, holding the wheel with a death grip. I believe I know what Ayrton Senna, my favorite Formula One driver of all time, felt like when he raced through the streets of Detroit. I was proud of myself since this was not something I do very often, and I was determined to see Rachel before her race with life was over.

I had a wonderful visit with Rachel and her family, went back through Detroit, Melvindale to pick up Beth, and headed back to Springfield, Missouri. Rachel is with the Lord, leaving her husband, Ron, and her three children. We will continue our conversation in heaven, girlfriend.

A couple of years before Rachel went to be with the Lord, she and her mother-in-law made Bill and me a quilt. We cherish that quilt, which remains on our bed. They wanted to do something for a missionary friend, a way of showing their love for us.

All of us gather precious friendships through the years. It is great to be in the presence of friends where you can be yourself, they can be themselves, and you feel safe with who they are. Another time, Rachel cross-stitched a poem for Bill and me to take to Brazil. Actually, I had given her the poem handwritten years before; she kept it because it said what we wanted to say to each other. I am not sure who the author is or even if it is complete, but it is beautiful.

> "Friendship is the comfort,
> The inexpressible comfort,
> Of feeling safe with a person.
> Having neither to weigh my thoughts
> Nor measure my words,
> But pouring all right out just as they are,
> Chaff and grain together,
> Certain that a faithful, friendly hand
> Will take and sift them,
> Keep what is worth keeping
> And with a breath of comfort
> Blow the rest away."

Make a memory today with a friend or family member. Most memories do not cost a fortune. Some of my sweetest memories were of homemade bread rising over the huge floor furnace, which took up a lot of space in the dining room. It was then baked until golden brown, where the aroma would pass through the second-floor vent to our bedrooms.

My dad told me the story of his cousins trying to listen in and the visitors not wanting to leave—really overstaying their visit—when one of the kids knocked over the chamber pot down to the furnace below—needless to say, the incident cleared them out quickly.

This vent on the second floor is also served for spying on Mom and Dad sitting together, eating the last piece of pie, or having coffee. There were not many leftovers with eight of us around; they deserved it. We could hear whispering conversations and hoped they weren't about us. We even watched Mom and Dad put presents under the Christmas tree from the vent, viewing the popcorn garland we made days before and paper chains and ornaments. Candy canes adorned every branch.

Make some memories for your children, grandchildren, family, and friends. Take some time with someone where you're not in a hurry, remembering it is an eternal investment. You will feel so rewarded. What we do now could affect this generation and those to come.

Hearing music may bring on a memory or a certain mood. While in our first few months in Brazil, our 4-year-old daughter April and I were going through a grocery store in the city of Campinas when she heard "Rhinestone Cowboy" playing over the radio. April looked up at me with her big brown eyes and mouth wide open and said, "They're playing Grandpa's song." It was so precious and heartwarming, but made me homesick for just a little while. That song took a four-year-old's heart back to the U.S. for just a moment in time.

Do you know your parents' favorite song, color, and food? Parents, do you know those things about your children? Don't let the years slip by without really knowing those people you care about; it is important to them that you notice those small things about them. As parents, it is important to make memories for our children. I regret learning this wonderful idea a little late because I know I could have done a better job making more wonderful memories for our children.

Life is hard, and the way we respond to life will depend on our relationship with Christ. Adults have attitudes, children have attitudes, the public has attitudes, and church members can surely have attitudes. Not all of these mindsets are godly in nature. In general, though, we are making memories for them, whether good or bad, hoping there are more good memories than bad. I have many wonderful memories of Flint, Michigan, and my early years in Springfield, Missouri, my real home. Who would not have lots to recall with a family of eight?

CHAPTER NINE: MAKING MEMORIES

Still, Still Green Bananas

There was not much to do on a day off in Pouso Alegre, Minas Gerais, but we did promise to fly a kite with April. The property for the camp had not been purchased yet, so we went to a friend's farm to have some family time. It was a beautiful day as we packed up the car.

Our first attempts at flying the kite were not successful. We did everything we could to get that kite to stay up but with no luck. Discouraged, we were ready to go home because we found nothing to use for the tail of the kite, thinking that might be the problem. Then a thought occurred to me, "I do have my hose on; that would probably make a good tail for the kite, huh!" This was a very difficult decision to make as I only had a couple of pairs from the States. Finally, after a moment of selfishness, the tug of war was over and the thought of making this little one happy won out.

There in the open field away from town, I took my Made in the USA nylons off, and believe it or not, they made a beautiful tail for the kite. It was a gorgeous sight as the radiant-colored, store-bought paper kite flew higher and higher, free as a bird. April was so excited and thrilled that Mom would give up her stockings to help make her kite fly. It was sure worth it after seeing the joy on April's face.

Little sacrifices can make a big difference in anyone's life, and we should be willing to make more of them. If we were to tell the truth, there are many more selfish moments than we realize. We comprehend later on that these moments are not sacrifices after all; they are memory making.

A few years later, our daughter decided to hide her allowance; she trusted no one, including her mother, dad, and little brother Robert. She carefully hid her billfold when no one else was looking. A few weeks and even months went by, and she had forgotten about her money. A year passed, and no mention of her billfold. Finally, April remembered her billfold but by this time couldn't remember where she placed it. She then began to blame everyone. She just knew her little brother found and spent it. Another year later, April happened to come upon her treasure. Believe it or not, it was right where she had left it, under the table leaf in the dining room. By this time, the money in her billfold was worthless; inflation had eaten up its value. In the end, her efforts were all in vain.

Sound familiar? So many of our efforts are done in vain and we are an exhausted, weary, and troubled bunch but shouldn't be. We would tire less and rest more if we would look to the Father and His ways. Just as April did, we hide precious riches, squander available riches, and waste so many costly resources. Life passes us by when we become so selfish, missing out on precious memories.

April trusted no one, was doubtful, and in the end, angry. We become like this, passing up so many opportunities where we could have been a blessing. There was worry about the loss, then there was the waste of her treasure. Anytime we put off investing in relationships, we miss blessings, great opportunities for growth, loss of valuable time, trust in one another, and loss of our treasures that would have been laid up for us.

It was fun listening to our children in their growing stages. When Robert was old enough and April would do something to irritate or take something away, he would say, "April Lloyd." When we heard this, we asked him why he called her April Lloyd, and he said, "That's what you call me when you're upset with me. Isn't that what you call everyone when you're mad?" We realized when we would be firmer with Robert, we changed the tone of our voice and used his middle name, Lloyd. Robert Lloyd is his full name. He thought he had to say the word Lloyd when he wanted to emphasize how mad he was, and I guess he was pretty mad at his sister. How funny and such a sweet memory.

◆ ◆ ◆ ◆ ◆

Our children will never forget the day we were driving away from our home at the campgrounds when I saw something move in the field. At that time, there were no buildings other than our home. Golden sunlight sparkled over the weed-colored field when I saw something or someone pop up and back down. I asked Bill to stop the car and let me see what it was, and of course, Bill, very cautious, reminded me not to get too close. Like a good detective, I walked over to the moving object slowly and cautiously, finding a painted grocery bag sticking out of the high weeds. Then all of a sudden, something jumped out at me, scaring me half to death. It was a young boy about eight years old, crying for me not to take his kite.

When I looked closer, I realized that this young boy was holding tightly to his homemade kite as if it was the largest treasure in the world.

As I approached, he began to hold his kite closer to him, crouching and hugging his knees, fearful of losing the only thing he had and begged me not to take it. Maybe this was all he had, the little he owned. Barefoot and bleeding, he began to tell me he had run away from home because his daddy would beat him. Most of his cuts were from barbed wire fences he dodged in the night. I really felt for him.

I really wanted to take this young one home, give him a good bath, good meal, and clean clothes, but Bill thought it might not be wise not knowing all the circumstances. Besides, if he was running away, someone was looking for him, so we put him and his kite in the car and headed for the city.

April and Robert froze on their side of the car, looking at this boy in such bewilderment, noticing that he still hung on very tight to his one possession. Bill stopped the car at the first policeman on the street and asked for his help. The officer knew immediately who the boy was and said it had not been the first time he had run away from home. As we approached the boy's home with the help of the officer, he became very fidgety. We asked for him to stay in the car for a minute as we wanted to talk to the boy's dad and the police officer. As we left the car, the boy leaped into the front seat and locked the car doors. Of course, Robert and April were stunned beyond belief.

Upon visiting with the father and the officer, we realized it was a very troubled home. We couldn't find out where the boy lived for all of the father's yelling at the child and felt it best for the young boy's sake not to push any further. We had no choice but to leave him with the officer and the boy's father, asking the officer to keep an eye out for the health of the child. We left that day overwhelmed with emotions, which became an important memory for our children for many years to come. We all wanted a happier ending for him but have prayed for this young boy and for his well-being in these years since; someone who stepped in and out of our lives so quickly, leaving such an unforgettable impression.

We all have good and bad times in our lives, and this is where we allow God to filter through those memories. Calling to remembrance can help or hinder in our walk with Christ. Some memories cause us to stumble as painful thoughts come to the surface. This is where I must give those painful thoughts to God, write down the date I gave it to Him, and when Satan brings it up to remind me once again, I tell him it's not mine anymore; take it up with my Father. You can't hurt me with this memory. Then I begin to praise the Lord. Philippians 4:8: "Think on these things..." Read that scripture carefully and then recall people, places, verses, and messages that filled your heart with gladness.

A precious friend of mine from Baptist Bible College days was dying of cancer. Rachel Mooney was from Michigan, which drew us together; we just seemed to hit it off along with a couple of other close friends in those days. Beth Adams, another dear friend, went with me to Michigan. Our plans were to drop Beth off in Melvindale, Michigan, then I would continue on to Flint the next morning, which would take me through Detroit.

◆◆◆◆◆

I went forward to accept Christ at an early age in Flint, Michigan, under the influence of my parents, Jewel Smith, Pastor Bobby Waddle, and others. Our family moved to Springfield, Missouri in 1959, where our pastor, Kenneth Gillming, dealt with me about assurance sometime later. He then baptized me, as well as a couple of my brothers and sisters, as charter members of Cherry Street. We were baptized at Seminole Baptist Church because, at that time, we had no baptismal in the garage where the church started.

My family lived in the house and paid half the rent, while the church congregation paid the other half of the rent using the garage for an auditorium. Our bedrooms, dining room, and living room were opened up and used as classrooms. Those were wonderful memories.

Mrs. Norma Gillming was my Sunday school teacher, and I remember winning a Bible for memorizing Romans 12.

Sometimes, Mrs. Gillming would let us have class outside under the trees when it was really warm. With no air conditioning, adventuring outside was a welcome treat. We soon discovered this was a no-no, as Mrs. Gillming would break out with poison ivy at the hint of a breeze from the woods behind the property.

Getting the house ready for Sunday school helped me in the preparation for new works in Brazil. It was a lot of fun with Ginger,

Keith, Kenny, and Mark living on the other side of the woods, a block over behind the church. We wore a pathway through the field to each other's houses. There were not too many dull moments between the Gillmings and the Stearns. Later, there came the McIntires, the Wilsons, the Dodsons, and more to bring Brother Gillming gray hair.

All in all, life's events mold and make us. I'm very thankful for the rich memories I have as a young child born in Michigan, raised in Springfield, Missouri, and growing up in Brazil. Yes, my growing-up years were my maturing with our Brazilian family. They will always have a special place in our hearts.

◆ ◆ ◆ ◆ ◆

If you want to know what a great barbecue is, go to Brazil; the folks in Cidade Foch know. Gerson is a precious man Bill led to Christ, eventually their children, and they were all baptized. His wife, Wilma, became one of my best friends and we hit it off. Their neighbors, Dilma and Walter, joined in and eventually Walter became a Christian, praise the Lord.

We all had reason to celebrate, so we celebrated around barbecues or churrasco with lombo, pork tenderloin, and beef kabobs, hump of the Brahma bull, rice, salads, and pastas. What a feast of food and fellowship around precious friends. Their homes were always welcoming places for us to crash any given day or hour.

We take you now to our work in Ouro Fino, 45 minutes away, which started in a family's open patio basement. Three or four families asked for us to come to start a new work in this area, and what a blessing it became. Such dear people gathered around Marina and Jayro's table, who poured out the best to us as servants of our Lord.

If we would go to Ouro Fino, they would take care of our Sunday meal and any needs we might have. Some opened their homes to have us for hot bread and coffee before the evening service. So many families always left their doors open to us. The Brazilians are very hospitable, loving, and generous people. Thank you for such precious memories.

Still, Still Green Bananas

The city of Pouso Alegre was the town where God first called us and where we set our stakes, going out from there to the surrounding area. This is where we had so many of our first experiences. Families there are still family to us, as well as in Cidade Foch and Ouro Fino; we hear from them often even now.

Our first experiences and best of memories were formed while in the city of Pouso Alegre, Minas Gerais, Brazil. Those families are still family to us, ones who suffered through language mistakes until we became fluent in Portuguese. Pastor Edivaldo and his wife Priscilla did a wonderful job for many years, serving beside us as coworkers. May God bless them richly as they continue to labor in Brazil.

Leonore is a very special member of our family who had such an influence on us as well as our children and taught me many things about Brazilian life. Her children were a bit older and loved entertaining ours, whether letting April roll their hair in curlers or taking Robert on bike rides. She and her girls taught April to sew, which she does beautifully because of the time spent with them.

Marcus, their son, and Simone, his wife, love the Lord and served as missionaries in the jungles for some time. Our children, now grown, still love her and appreciate the devotion and love her and her family have shown to them, the Lord, and others.

One of our favorite places to eat in Pouso Alegre knew us so well from Sunday visits that we could hear the waiters say, "The Americans are here; bring out the ice, forget the peas, and bring out the ketchup." Ice was not normally served to the Brazilians as long as the sodas were good and cold, and peas decorated many dishes to give color, and ketchup on fries was an American thing.

At another cozy eatery that we had a chance to visit in our beginning weeks in our new town, I asked for ketchup, and the waiter took off his apron, went to the grocery store, and bought a bottle of ketchup for our fries. They do love to please. Waiters are common, not waitresses, so it seems more formal even in the simplest of places.

One precious memory I have of that first restaurant is mentioning the peas; I remember Bill signaling to the waiter after our meal. I thought he was asking for the bill. The waiter came across the restaurant with a chocolate cake and the strangest candle I had ever seen. In the middle of the cake was a 40-watt light bulb! You guessed it. It was my 40th birthday, and the whole restaurant knew about it. That's Bill Levergood—full of surprises. But I got him back on his 60th. But one thing was different: his 60-watt light bulb lit up, my 40-watt did not. Reminiscences! Make some memories; you will be a richer person for it.

Still, Still Green Bananas

When We Were Young

Many things kept us out of mischief
When we were young.
Like stilts that made us feel so tall
We could almost touch the sky.
There were baseball cards
Of our favorite team
Together with bubblegum
We chewed by the wad.

Then there were suckers that lasted all day,
That's when a nickel went a long way.
The Maypole was a lot of fun
When we got it going fast;
The secret was to run real hard
And lift our feet up last.
Mother May I, jumping rope and
Red Rover send him on over,
Were always Saturday games.

We loved playing in the autumn leaves;
Gathering, raking, and piling them
Just to mess them up again.
Winter came was a smash
Bringing snow that sure would last.
Snowball fights were so much fun
Until hit by, head-on.

We left impressions in the snow
Spreading angel wings throughout the yard
Giving appearance of an angelical choir
Made by us who were no saints.

A snowman whom we did build
Became a special sort of friend.
He could not stay too long to play
As spring waited around the bend
To melt him fast away.
We weren't sad for he promised to return

Still, Still Green Bananas

And that he does each year without fail
Bringing with him those memories
Of when we were young,
A reenactment of those early years.

© by Carol Levergood

Days Gone By

I recall those things
Which brought joy to me
Like fresh strawberries in the field
And rhubarb as wild as its taste.
Then there were daisies, wildflowers
And dandelions, that when in seed,
Blew off into the wind.

Or those woods by the side of the house
That seemed so friendly by day
And so eerie by night;
Full of mysteries whispering, the
Trees between themselves
A language that only childish fear
Would understand.
There was an outhouse that stood out back,
Which became a target at Halloween
It served when we were playing nearby
If an urgent call became the theme.
Then there was the shed
That led to the kitchen
With green switches hanging there in shame,
Not liking much their job,
Pouting they were sorely famed.
They had heard the statement often said,
"It hurts me more than it hurts you."
Words hard to believe
When the meetings they did witness
In the shed so dark and gloom.

I recall at an early age
The bottled milk that came to our kitchen door.
Regular or chocolate
In a wire basket on the floor.
It was finally understood how
Cows gave chocolate milk;
The color of the cow
Had lots to do with that IM sure.

Still, Still Green Bananas

I've just wondered,
I've not really understood
Why a black cow can't give coffee
I would surely think he could.

I remember chocolate syrupy fudge
That we lay too harden like taffy
In the freshly fallen snow.
Or graham crackers and chocolate bars
With marshmallows melted o'er the cooling coals
Of the chimneyed barbecue pit
That stood proudly made of stone.
Yes, those days are days gone by
For many years have passed since then,
And as the fond memories tried to slip away
I gather them back again
As if a yo-yo still in play.

© by Carol Levergood

This page is dedicated to those wonderful friends and Christian families who have lost loved ones on the highways of Brazil. We have wonderful memories of them, who now experience that glorious hope in our Lord and Savior Jesus Christ. They continue to bombard our hearts with "saudades," meaning a real empty spot hard to fill, where once they faithfully served alongside us.

One Christmas Eve, we received news that little eight-year-old Tiago Guimaraes died in a car accident coming from the city of São Paulo, heading for Pouso Alegre. Tiago had to be buried within 24 hours, as was the custom. Hearts were breaking, and they were questioning and expressing their feelings for the family, which they themselves did not fully understand. The white casket held this beautiful boy who meant so much to all of us.

Christmas Day will always be remembered as the day we buried little Tiago. Not long after, his father, in desperation, tried to hang himself. But today, he is strong, loves the Word, and leaves Tiago in the hands of the Lord. He and Albete have two handsome grown sons who love the Lord. God bless you, precious friends, as you walk with Him and hold that "hope" of one day seeing Tiago again. Not that hope of maybe, but of knowing for sure.

Gleide Diefrich, a godly, beloved, and upright woman who loved testifying about her Jesus and was not afraid to stand up for Him, died in a bus accident, leaving six children—a tragedy for the town of Ouro Fino. Carl Taylor, a New Tribes Missionary, was killed in a car accident along with his granddaughter, another missionary, and a college student. Gilsane, a young lady from our second work in Ouro Fino, was also seriously hurt in this accident. She has since recuperated, married, and has a family. Pastor Clarette and Margarida, dear friends and a faithful, godly pastor and his wife, were involved in an accident on the highway. Clarette died on the side of the highway between Campinas and Pouso Alegre; his wife shortly after in the hospital. Their daughters were with him when he was taken home to be with the Lord.

One day, we will see all of these precious people and many more who have passed on since. Aren't you glad God prepared a home in heaven for those who would accept Him as the only one to forgive sins? And accept His cleansing work that day on Calvary? Thank you, Jesus. Amen, and amen.

CHAPTER TEN: TROLLS, GIANTS, AND MOUNTAINS

Still, Still Green Bananas

As a child in Michigan, I remember my older brothers and sisters playing a game where they would say the troll would get us as we passed over to the other side of our make-believe bridge. I was so afraid, taking everything literally then. In my mind, the trolls were make-believe giants, fearsome, ugly monsters that kept me afraid.

There have been many giants in my life since then, mostly in my imagination, camouflaged in "what if?" I am sure you have faced some other kinds of giants in your life. In Joshua and Caleb's case, the giants were very real, as we know from the other ten spies who scouted the land God said to claim. They were scared to death at the thought of continuing their journey, but Joshua and Caleb felt that with God's help, the giants could be conquered.

In my case, the giants of self-confidence and self-esteem were always lurking around the corner. Why did I need to have a boost of an encouraging word or a pat on the back? The giant of failure made friends with self-confidence and self-esteem, adding to the disaster. Sometimes, I would not try anything new for fear of failing. These giants, even though they were in my thoughts and imagination, became real, and the thought of failure was just as real as if I had failed. I was sure the whole world knew when in reality, it was never as big and horrible as I had envisioned. But my mind's eye visualized and magnified the situation many times over.

I finally understood, not just read, Philippians 4:8. I knew the verse by heart but felt it was written for a Christian rebelling against God with ungodly thoughts, although not accepting myself as God made me and accepting His unconditional love was ungodly. I must love myself as God loves me. I had to learn how to think on God's truth, honestly seeing myself as God sees me. My own expectations of myself and of others were so high they became unreachable.

In our ministry now of more than 40 years, we have had many mountains to climb and valleys to pass through, but this mountain I would like to tell you about is a very special one. Bill and I were interested in finding the right property to build the camp a number of years ago. We found one that really grabbed us, with the land sprawled to the foot of the mountains behind it. We started praying that God would give us this beautiful property with the mountains as the backdrop.

Each time we passed on the highway, we just knew in our hearts that the mountain was ours, and we claimed it. I just knew that God would see fit for us to have this land. I would say to our children, April and Robert, "There's my mountain! God gave it to me, my own personal mountain." Robert would say, "Mom, it's not your mountain. You did not pay for it. It's not on the camp property." Then I would say, "I know, son, but as long as I can enjoy it from a kitchen window, as long as it brings joy to me and makes me think more about my creator, then it's mine."

I believe Robert understood what I was talking about. He understood that it didn't have to be on our property for us to enjoy it. As Robert became older, he would say, "Hey, Mom, isn't your mountain pretty today?" When we would arrive from a trip and were closer to the camp, the kids would look for the tip of the mountain and know we were closer to home. "There's your mountain, Mom!" I guess we finally convinced him.

All of this reminds me of a song I used to sing as a child: (chorus)

> He owns the cattle on a thousand hills
> The wealth in every mine
> He owns the rivers and the rocks and rills
> The sun and stars that shine
> Wonderful riches more than tongue can tell
> They are my Father's so they're mine as well
> He owns the cattle on a thousand hills
> I know that He will care for me.

A neighbor lady and friend told us she could hear the young people sing all the way to her house on the far side of the mountain. She said her family would sit on the front porch and listen to the choruses sung by the many voices present in the chapel. This woman came to know Christ as her Savior in our car in front of the marketplace sometime later. She said that she was afraid of dying but what an opportunity to show her the Lord. Since this time, she has gone home to be with the Lord. Praise His name. We are to sing His praises and lift Him up.

"O magnify the Lord with me, and let us exalt His name together." Psalm 34:3.

"The Lord liveth; and blessed be my rock; and let the God of my salvation be exalted." Psalm 18:46.

God gave us that mountain to conquer for Him, but that would be only one of many mountains. Years later, a young man began working for us at the camp who had accepted Christ many years before in one of the Saturday Bible classes. God laid on my heart the desire to have a Saturday Bible club for the kids on that mountain years before. At least 11 children that I know of accepted Christ through that Bible study. My prayer is that the seed planted through the years will grow and bring forth much fruit. I pray that the Holy Spirit will continue to work in the lives of each soul and that they will not keep it to themselves.

What mountain have you claimed? What giants have you taken on? Was it in the strength of the Lord? Oh, that we might be like Joshua and Caleb in recognizing the giants. Don't act like they are not there; you'll just be fooling yourself. Recognize them and then face them head-on in God's power and might. He promises He will not ask you to do something that He will not enable you to do. Too many times, I went in my own strength, saying, "Come on, Lord! Let's go get 'em!" Instead of allowing Him to lead, giving the marching orders.

Bill's family faced the giant of war, but not even World War II could keep God's plan from being fulfilled. Dad Levergood was done with his basic training and had gone for his overseas physical when he received the news that he had only six months to live. The doctors said that his heart was very bad and that he could take a desk job or be sent home to be with his family for the rest of his days. He chose to go home to be with his family.

The rest of Dad's unit was sent over to Germany, most of them wiped out in the Battle of the Bulge. The irony of all of this was that Bill's dad lived another 44 years. Bad heart, huh? God spared Walter Levergood. God knew what was going on, and there are no coincidences with Him.

My husband Bill was born five years later. If Dad had gone to war, he most likely would have been killed at the Battle of the Bulge, and Bill Levergood would not have been, would not have been a missionary to Brazil, and I certainly would not have been married to this wonderful man. We are so thankful for God sparing Walter Levergood.

Bill and I count it a privilege to have served our Lord alongside the precious people of Brazil. Those experiences make us who we are today. As I have already said, "I was born in Michigan, raised in Springfield, and grew up in Brazil." All of the mountains and valleys were to lift and strengthen us and never once used to try to defeat us. I failed many tests, wondering if God really knew what He was doing. We need to face the giants as David did head-on, pushing the doubts and fears aside.

Remember, fear will paralyze you. I know! Faith, on the other hand, will make you soar above the circumstances and lift you on to victory. Victory is not fireworks; it is knowing you went through the fire unsinged in God's strength, not yours.

When our family left Brazil, we realized how much we were bonded with the Brazilian people. Packing up, selling things or giving them away, some of our Brazilian family said, "All these things we bought from you, or you have given to us, are yours if you just come back." That meant so much to us. Every meal was taken care of for the last couple of weeks before leaving, and what really touched our hearts was the scene at the marketplace. Merchants, customers, and townspeople not of our faith said their goodbyes with hugs, waves, and soccer shirts for each of us. Unbelievers were left with the seed, the Word of God, by the example of Christian Americans. Some heard the Gospel message and received it, while others did not, blinded by traditions.

We begin a new chapter in our lives and now have other mountains to climb. The giant of fear pops up its ugly head from time to time, but now, with the imagination under godly control, the giants don't look so big after all. God wants us to learn self-control, even when it concerns fear. When I show fear, I show very little faith. Self-control is one of the fruits of the Spirit in Galatians 5:22-23.

We have a new bunch of people to love and work with, just as we did for 12 years at Dunnegan Bible Baptist Church. Now on staff at Cherry

St. Baptist Church (coming around full circle), we work, worship, and serve together with the wonderful staff. Bill has been at Baptist Bible College for 18 years now.

We are waiting and anticipating great things from God as we all continue to carry the good news as He has commanded. May we all be found faithful, serving Him who so much deserves our praise.

Still, Still Green Bananas

CHAPTER ELEVEN: TERMITES, BATS, FROGS, AND MORE

Still, Still Green Bananas

Huge mounds take over acres and acres of land in the state of Minas Gerais, Brazil. Most Brazilians call these mounds "praga" or a plague. They are built by termites, mud termites, and if allowed, will literally devour the land, making it nonproductive for planting or grazing. Our family has seen some banks as high as our waists peaking at the top. It is possible for one acre of land to have hundreds of them.

When they are dry, they are almost as hard as cement. The termites inside do not bring the dirt from other places; they take it out of the earth below and mix it with their saliva, which hardens like cement. The hollow mounds then make a good habitat for snakes to take advantage of in the winter for warmth. But if the heaps are hard, how do the snakes get inside?

This takes yet another critter to make the holes. The woodpecker, called Xa-Xa, is what I call a cement pecker because he goes after the mounds and chimneys made of brick. Actually, he is looking for food, bugs like the termites. Take them, please, take every one of them termites; they are a plague also. The vicious circle continues—the more termites, the more woodpeckers, and then more snakes around.

Bill and the workers tried to keep termites off Camp Rainbow's property by poisoning, burning, or smoking them out, but to no avail. Talk about a constant battle never completely won. We finally learned to search for any mounds beginning to form and try to be rid of them while they were still small. That should be the practice of a Christian: deliberately catching the small seeds planted in our minds and in our hearts before they become destructive. Yes, a great devotional or illustration to be used in our lives, don't you think? Life is full of opportunities to learn if we are willing to pay attention, even in God's creation.

The Tiziu Bird

The tiny Tiziu Bird is a fascinating South American bird almost extinct today. A person could be fined or jailed for hunting or wounding a Tiziu bird. Many times as I would tire of washing dishes, ironing clothes, or washing the big L-shaped veranda with the squeegee, I would try to remember this bird.

I often saw the Tiziu from off the porch or from the kitchen, looking over the fields and the mountain behind our house. Sitting on one of the fence posts that divide the property from our neighbors, the tiny critter started his debut. There, he jumped up and down, up and down into the air in a precise rhythm. He never seemed to tire of the endless springing, almost as perfect as an ice skater landing on the ice after a swirl in the air.

The fence post is only so big, and the diameter is no bigger than the palm of a man's hand. He never once lost his balance, was always on target, and was proud to be doing just that. Each time he jumped, he sang a note high to low, high to low, never changing, hour after hour.

How many of us have heard our children say, "I'm bored. There's nothing to do"? Sometimes, we feel we have a monotonous, boring life and feel like we are in a rut. We do tire of the same thing every day, and life can seem without variety. Maybe there is something you can do about it, like singing while doing dishes or listening to uplifting music, or how about praising God? Look for small changes to be made to make your job more enjoyable, change an attitude, or pray for someone else to change theirs. I thought to myself, "How could this little creature be happy doing the same thing day after day?" Little did this awesome creation of God know that in doing just that, he was a blessing to me.

What seemed monotonous to me could be considered consistency to others. Someone is paying attention to you and your actions. How we look at things depends a lot upon our attitude and what we tell ourselves from biblical standards. The book of Psalms and Proverbs tells us how to be joyful and what things we should think about so that our thoughts may be pleasing to God. We all need variety, but when we become weary from continued sameness, we then lose our perspective and purpose. Keep your eyes on your goals. If you do not have any, then set some.

This little bird continued on the post for the longest time, then flew away to rest upon another, only to start his pattern of jumps and springs again. Let us be more like the Tiziu Bird, doing whatever we do with a good attitude, counting our blessings, and praising our Creator.

Still, Still Green Bananas

O Alegre Tiziu

O Tiziu
Pula pra lá
Pula pra cá,
Nunca se cansa
Dos pulos no ar.
Ele sempre acerta
O seu pulo na cerca
Com tanto orgulho
No mesmo lugar,
Nunca se reclama
De pular e cantar.

Nós não cansamos
Do nosso dia a dia?
Vamos fazer igual ao Tiziu
Fazendo tudo
Com muita alegria.

© by Carol Levergood

Another interesting creature we find is the XÃ-XÃ bird. We call it the cement woodpecker because he only pecks at blocks or bricks—making holes as big as cereal bowls—at least my cereal bowl! We would shoot the BB gun around them to shoo them off. The stack had several holes, and when we lit the fireplace—our source of heat in the living area—there were several streams of smoke billowing out. From a distance, the chimney stack looked more like a stuttering Indian smoke signal.

The holes in the chimney caused further complications. Our family was seated together in the living room when I looked over and saw a bat on the wall. He had taken advantage of entering the holes prepared by the XÃ-XÃ, covering himself in soot from the chimney. Of course, I pointed this bat out to Bill, who gave me this look of, "So…?" He then says, "Get a pail and I'll nab him."

I rushed the pail to him, but in the meantime, Bill grabbed the hand-stitched pillow my mom made and smashed the bat against the wall, soot everywhere. Distracted by the soccer game, Bill let the bat slip from his grasp, sliding down on his pant leg. When I pointed it out to him, Mr. Macho himself started dancing a jig even I can't describe (He did dance like a girl, though). My dad thought that was where the Brazilian Lambada originated. I can laugh about it now, but it took a while to clean the black mess off the pillow and wall; never a dull moment with Bill. OK! OK! I wouldn't trade him.

◆◆◆◆◆

I was sitting pretty and privately on the throne, minding my own business, when I looked down beside me. My eyes met with this huge furry creature, which I had seen many times on the road but never up close and personal. Without waiting a second longer, I was on the small countertop, spread in the sink, occupying the whole perimeter of the basin. That was a sight to see. It was a huge tarantula that probably came from the market wrapped with the fruit and vegetables or from the mountains behind us.

I let Bill and half the neighborhood know I was in danger, or at least thought I was. Although the most danger I was probably in was getting stuck in the sink. Tarantulas can make you really ill, but for the most part, they are not fatal. I just know he did not like me, and I sure did not like him and was positive he had a family in the house somewhere. So the frantic search began for any little furry creatures. I did feel very uneasy for the next couple of days until I was able to get my mind off the intruder.

Cooking at the camp was quite an experience, not that I had the experience to get the job; it came with the ministry. I decided to delve thoroughly into cookbooks and learn firsthand from my dear Brazilian family. I would eat at their homes, love their food, and then ask for recipes. I love cooking, which helped me with the ministry set for the years ahead.

The campgrounds could be reserved for any day of the year except Christmas and New Year's Day. As the popularity of the camp grew, we often had two camps a month throughout the year. Some reserved the grounds for concentrated studies, conferences, pastors' retreats, and even choir seminars. Three of my helpers accepted Christ in that kitchen. One sweet lady accepted the Lord while peeling potatoes with me. It is a wonderful thing to know that God hears our desire to accept Him anywhere, even in the kitchen.

Camps were exciting because of revival in the hearts of the young people and because many came to know Christ as their Savior. At our first camp, we invited a special guest, a 12-year-old girl, younger than we would normally allow at a high school camp. During one of the meetings, she ran to her dorm in tears, so I followed her to see if I could help. She related to me that she had recently visited a palm reader who showed her a very bleak future where she would be forsaken by her friends.

This young lady had just been released from the hospital after trying to take her life. That day on her bunk bed, I was able to lead her to the Lord. She found the Savior who could show her what a full and victorious life she could have in Him. I told her no palm reader was needed; just open the Word and see that Jesus loves you.

Eleven years later, we saw her marry a wonderful young man, with Bill performing the wedding. Praise the Lord. This young lady's uncle took her to camp because of concern for her soul and her happiness. Her uncle Joao accepted Christ through the influence of the SMITE Teams from Liberty University a few years before. What a blessing they were to our town. Joao taught catechism in the Catholic Church, but the next day after accepting Christ, he turned in his keys to the church. Of course, they did not take it very well, but he responded in this way, "I have learned more about Christ in one evening than I have all these years serving at the Catholic Church." He found the truth that Jesus saves. The many idols were dismissed from his life, and until this day, Jesus Christ is still supreme.

The Bible says there is one mediator between God and men, the man Christ Jesus, found in 1 Timothy 2:5. He simplified salvation for us, and all we want to do is complicate the absolute solution. Jesus is sufficient as we find in John 14:6 and John 3:16.

◆◆◆◆◆

Carnival camp arrived this year with a bang, and I was already in the kitchen preparing lasagna for our supper meal. Leaving the water to boil, I left the stove for just a moment to do something with the salads. Placing the noodles in the water, I stirred them to make sure they didn't stick together. I talked to a few of the campers, then went to stir again, and to my surprise, I found a frog stiffened in a backstroke position that would have made our Olympic swimmers proud. I began to take the pot to rinse the noodles with freshwater and start again. Bill, with his sense of humor, said, "Leave it there! Frog legs are a delicacy, and after all, it is fresh meat."

I still have no idea where that frog came from, but he sure got a surprise. I wondered whether he had been in the pan from the beginning, and if that is the case, he probably thought it was a nice swimming place—cool water to begin with. He probably just rested and enjoyed the cool temperature of the water, not feeling the temperature change. His body adjusted with the rising temperature, not really noticing the change until it was too late. If he wasn't there in the beginning, he probably just jumped one time too many right into the kettle. I had to use the noodles; I just didn't tell the campers.

Christians jump into things too fast, not really thinking about the consequences of their actions. Or some may have a lukewarm attitude, pulled in and out of fellowship, not even realizing they have been so cool toward God's Word, work, and fellowship. By the time they realize, they have been scarred, burned, or not in any position to back out.

Many young people think, "If I could get out of this house, or if I could marry him, I would be happy; at least I would get away from home." Running from one situation into another usually doesn't solve anything. Working through relationships helps to grow, then we become ready for another. I am not talking about an abusive situation; I am, however, talking about those grinding, hard-to-get-along-with kind. Relationships take time to build. There is no magic involved; just thinking more of others and less of us.

The second thing I see in the frog incident, which I touched on slightly, is a heart turning cold by a subtle day-by-day, week-by-week giving in to the world's influence. The frog is much like some who dabble their feet in the world but, as he found out, the heat was on. Today, Christians seem to think they do not want to be put into a Christian mold, so they sit on the fence, a very dangerous place for the children of God.

All of us, no matter how we dress or act, are identifying ourselves with someone or some group. But the Word of God still remains the same. Be what God wants you to be, not what mankind thinks you should be for you to make an impact on this world. Your cool dress and your new upbeat fashion working with young people will not speak or do the job of the Holy Spirit. So many Christians have been fooled by this notion. Ask God to convict you, leaving aside your opinions and assumptions. But there is one more step—listen and obey the wooing of the Holy Spirit—follow through.

The generation before you and the one before that may have failed in many ways, but like them, you are responsible to do the right thing when you know what is right. Like the molds we felt were forced to fit in can also be dangerous because they are manmade, but some were not really molds; they were morals. They were people who were trying to hold back the world's influence from degrading rapidly, even though they may have gone about it in the wrong way. But all of us will be held accountable for how we handled the Word of God, which has not changed through all the ages. Man's interpretation has changed according to what he wants to interpret, but we must heed God's Word whether we like it or not.

Practicing moderation in all of our ways is Christ-like. The unbelievers here, as well as in Brazil, are weary of seeing hypocritical Christians who look spiritual but do not pay their bills, have bad credit, and have a bad testimony in their neighborhoods. Do you see where we, as Christians, can do more harm than good? Why do we believe we're getting away with something when God is very much aware of our actions? Individually, in our hearts, we need to look and verify the motives for our actions. Taking advantage of a church's goodness, kindness, and help is taking advantage of God. If we can help ourselves, then we must.

Today's society is a society of entitlement. Today's society is bombarded with the world's opinions and philosophies. Today's society would just as soon turn from God than to claim Him because it's too hard to be called a Christian. May that not be said of any of us in the days ahead as we wait for His return. Like in Braveheart, pick up the flag, pick up the banner, and carry on, pressing forward to accomplish what is necessary to keep God's Word going out to all nations. May God bless each one who has read this testimony, and may we all rejoice in God's healing power in every relationship that touches our lives.

There will always be plagues, big and small, in our lives—something or someone that digs at your very being. How do we live with these situations? By giving them to the Lord or releasing them, saying, "I am tired of trying to change things, tired of trying to change people. I give this situation or this person to You, Father. You change what is necessary to change in their lives, and I will take my hands off, allowing You to work. It may take time, days, and weeks, but I am willing to allow You to work. Change me where I need to change. Help me not to place my expectations of others so high. When others fail me, teach me to forgive just as I want to be forgiven when I have failed."

Let the Lord convict those people of changes that need to take place in their lives, stand back, and watch the Lord work. A lot depends on his or her desire to change, but at least you are free of the burden of trying to change them. A load should be lifted. A suggestion here is to write down the date, for example, 1/12/95, that you gave that difficult situation or person to the Lord. When thoughts come to worry and upset you again and again, you just tell Satan it is no longer your problem, that you gave it to the Lord, so he is to take it up with Him. It belongs to the Lord; you left it at the foot of the cross. It's no longer yours. The old devil takes pride in reminding us when we have failed, but God's forgiveness is eternal. Don't try to take it back. When you do that, you are telling Him the work on Calvary wasn't enough. God forbid.

We can't stuff everyone in the pantry to ripen like we did with the green bananas at the beginning of the book. I know we would like to leave some difficult people in there indefinitely, I'm sure, but that's not possible. Do you know how many pantries that would take? So logically, God's way is the best way to work on relationships rather than to run from them. That means working on those hurts, fears, and disappointments.

I pray this book will be of benefit to you, perhaps sparing you my experience of panic, anxiety, and depression. I have come a long way and have found that I have to take life one day at a time, which God intended for us. Never lose hope! God is always present. I pray that God will send someone to lift you up, walk with you, and encourage you in this life's journey. Friends are important.

There will always be ups and downs, but with the tools I have acquired, I hope that I'm able to look at circumstances and situations with a healthier balance of judgment and emotions. Some of us can easily imagine the worst, but remember God wants us to think on those things of good report. On my wall, I have a plaque that reads, "Do not be afraid of tomorrow, God is already there." Amen and amen.

Still, Still Green Bananas

Ending Prayer

In the name of Your Son, Jesus Christ, I thank You for Your eternal presence. Help us to look past our iniquities and what we are not and look to who You are! Ripen, mature, and grow me that I may walk in Your ways. Father, help me! I am still green!

Still, Still Green Bananas

The Almost Forgotten Song

They wept when they remembered Zion,
The children of Israel.
The land they loved so much
Seemed so distant in their dreams.

The memories
Brought sorrow to their hearts.
Something that should bring joy
Brought bitterness that marked.
Hidden by the veil of sin
That sadly led them there.
Not even the riches of Babylon
Could erase memoirs so dear.

The people began to cry, "The song is not the same."
It's lost its message
Somewhere between
The freedom we knew
And the present state of doom.

Then caught in a pillow of contentment
Now to be blown away
By the wind of despair
Whatever hope was left.
They did not sing the Lord's song
When it was close to them.
They were slowly forgetting the tune
And how it must be sung.
Then someone spoke aloud,
"We must not forget the music,
We must continue to sing.
Our children must know our God
In whom we do believe."

Than at last a courageous voice began to sing
And then another sang along.
Seventy years of silence broke
And a muffled sound became a song.
Praise be to Jehovah-Jireh
The mighty God of Abraham,
Isaac and Jacob;
O Holy El Shaddai.

© by Carol Levergood

Still, Still Green Bananas

One Last Glance

Sodom and Gomorrah
Were two cities of a kind.
Twin cities
Infamous for their sinful ways
Ungodly and defiled.
An escape from the fate of destruction
The righteous Father had denied.

Lot's wife full of uncertainty
Found hesitancy in her steps;
Half stopping in her way
Her heart betwixt,
She pondered in her mind
Those orders very clearly defined.

Her heart pounded and tugged within
As if a child wanting her own way.
With the odor of sulfur in the air,
Her senses were quickened
Arousing her curiosity as well.

Those very hesitant steps
Full of self-will, shaped in iniquity
Were then to be sculptured
By the Creator himself;
As the price of disobedience
Would determine her destiny.

In unbelief she slowly turned.
Hearing the crackling of the burning wood
She viewed the flames and ashes
Sandwiched between the thick dark clouds.
There she viewed righteous judgment on display.

Tasting bitterness, hearing screams of despair
She stopped abruptly in her tracks;

Still, Still Green Bananas

In that final twist of a turn
The merciful grace of God was spurned,
As she began to feel her body change
To a lifeless pillar of salt.

© by Carol Levergood

Sweet Bullets

"A good name is more desirable than great riches; to be esteemed is better than silver or gold." Proverbs 22

Walter Levergood was called up from the National Guard during the Detroit riots in 1967. Leaving home, he was gone for several days when he was allowed to return home for an hour, eat a meal, and see his family. Tired and hungry, he began to unload his gun for safety purposes, of course. He had been placing the bullets in his shirt pocket when plop went one of the bullets into the applesauce. That's all it took for him to earn the nickname of Barney Fife among the immediate family.

When Bill told me that story, I just laughed because I could picture this happening. Plus, it doesn't take much, does it, to receive a name for what we did or said? People can be cruel, but in this case, it brought back a good time—a memory and laughter. Some nicknames are cruel and are meant to hurt; laughing at the person and not the incident can be harmful. But in this case, the incident was the target of fun. He even accepted his Barney Fife nickname.

We have given names to different Bible personages, such as Doubting Thomas, when in actuality it is not given in the Bible. The Bible says the disciple doubted... Then there was Laughing Sarah; to bear a child at her age? Then there is Barnabas in Acts 4. He is called...Son of Consolation or encouragement—wow, what a great nickname.

What do people think of us, or what comes to your mind when you think of a person—friend or foe? Better than that, what do others think of us? "I don't care!" We might say that, but deep down, we do care what others think, and we should to a point. We may have caused people to talk, and whether we like it or not, we have to take some of that as part of the consequences.

Let's pray that most will wrap their arms around us, lift us up, and help us along. That's what I would want if it were me facing consequences. If we deserve it or not, give it all to Jesus and let Him weigh the choices those people made also, right or wrong. Whatever, I just hope they are sweet bullets in the applesauce sort of things—when we have to face the music. Green or not, here we come!

ABOUT THE AUTHOR

Who is the Banana Lady?

Her name is Carol Levergood. She is a CLASSeminar member with Florence Littauer and is likened to a modern-day Carmen Miranda. She proposes a series of books with a unifying banana theme, wherein humorous anecdotes segue into meditative thoughts that touch the mind and spirit.

I'm Going Bananas and *A Banana With No "Peel"* are unlike anything you have read before. Other written manuscripts include *Fried Green Bananas*, *Piece of Cake*, *Son Ripened*, and *Honey, Please Stop for Directions*, a women's directional devotions study guide. Each devotional book is around 150-170 pages in length.

Who would have dreamed God would use green bananas to teach her one of life's greatest lessons: the growing and maturing process? This process does not have to be as painful as we make it. Like the green bananas we placed in our pantry to aid in the ripening process, Carol too was behind in her personal ripening and maturing as a Christian. Yes, she says she is still green, but one day soon, she will be as ripe and mature as Jesus intended her to be.

She is a pastor's wife and former missionary to Brazil. After 21 years as missionaries, they returned to Missouri, where her husband Bill became Senior Pastor of the Dunnegan Bible Baptist Church outside Bolivar for 12 years. He is Dean of Men at the Baptist Bible College in Springfield, Missouri, where Bill has worked for over 26 years. They are both graduates of Baptist Bible College and have been serving on staff at Cherry Street Baptist Church for over 16 years.

Since the revision of this book, her husband, Bill Levergood, has gone to be with the Lord. She states, "He has left a gigantic hole in my life, but each day I feel God's presence filling it with His mercy and grace."
05-29-24.
His funeral was 06-06-24.
"See you soon, Sweetheart. Until then."

Still, Still Green Bananas

Still, Still Green Bananas

Still, Still Green Bananas

Made in the USA
Monee, IL
29 October 2024

68908044R10074